Prayer That Changes Things

Presented to:

_____

From:

_____

Unless otherwise indicated, all Scripture quotations are taken from the *King James Version* of the Bible.

Some Scripture quotations have been italicized and underlined by the author for emphasis.

"Some Scripture quotations marked AMP are taken from *The Amplified ® Bible*, Copyright © 1954, 1958, 1962, 1964, 1965, 1987 by The Lockman Foundation. Used by permission." (www.Lockman.org)

Other Scriptures references are from the following sources: Scripture quotations marked (NIV) are taken from the HOLY BIBLE, NEW INTERNATIONAL VERSION ®. *NIV* ®. Copyright © 1973, 1978, 1984 by International Bible Society. Used by permission of Zondervan. All rights reserved worldwide.

Prayers and confessions are paraphrased from these versions unless otherwise stated.
Cover design © 2016 by Amy Eagan, Romero McBride

All rights reserved. No portion of this book may be reproduced, stored in a retrieval system, or transmitted in any form or by any means-electronic, mechanical, photocopy, recording, scanning, or any other-except for brief quotations in critical reviews or articles, without the prior written permission of the publisher.

Prayer That Changes Things
Copyright © 2016 by Beverly P. McBride
ISBN:0692446540-ISBN-13:978-0692446546

Acknowledgements

I would first like to make known publicly my adoration for my Daddy, Jesus by saluting, honoring, thanking, praising, and worshipping Him in the accomplishment of His finished product.
"God gave the word and great was the company of those that published it."
Psalms 68:11 KJV

To Romero, my one and only son, I sincerely appreciate and embrace your unswerving prayers, your patience, your excitement, and all of the continued support you have given me upon completing this assignment.

To each of my family members, I say God loves you more than you could ever imagine, ask or think!

To both of my Pastors, Dr. Creflo and Taffi Dollar, thank you for your faithfulness shown towards God by your example demonstrated, which has truly made a mark in my life that has inspired me to step up, to step out, and into what God has called, charged, ordained and anointed me to do.

A special thank you to Sherry Sanders, Louise Tipler, Dr. Wanda White, Dr. and Mrs. William Lamb, to both Mr. and Mrs. Kent Lovelace, Angela Whitehead, to Amy Eagan, and also to Tristin Bates, I decree that the exceeding greatness of His power continually be yours!

Table of Contents

Acknowledgements v

Preface vii

Dedication viii

About the Author 1

Practicing the Presence of God 2

Reaching Towards Heaven 37

Almighty God 72

A Yielded Vessel 97

Having Great Expectation 128

Remarkable Results 170

Preface

*This dynamic book that you have in your hands on **"Prayer That Changes Things,"** I believe will be the most powerful tool that a believer can have and utilize in order to successfully triumph in every endeavor of life as it relates to "prayer." For many, prayer is regarded as a strict mystical ritual that is passionately believed to be set aside, reserved and practiced religiously only for the godly devout Christian. While on the other hand this is by far undoubtedly untrue and illusory.*

This book is specifically designed to vividly show, to reveal and truthfully examine closely through the Word of God that **PRAYER** *is:*

- **P**... Practicing
- **R**... **R**eaching and **R**elating To The
- **A**... Almighty God Through
- **Y**... Yielding and
- **E**... Expecting
- **R**... **R**emarkable **R**esults

DEDICATION

It is my desire to dedicate this amazing book to all whom have made Jesus as Lord over their lives in hopes that they may learn to develop a much more profound and closer relationship with Him through the proven pathway in prayer. I release my faith with yours now to declare Ephesians 1: 17-19 over your life ...

"That the God of our Lord Jesus Christ, the Father of glory, may give you the spirit of wisdom and revelation in the knowledge of Him and that the eyes of your understanding be enlightened; that ye may know what is the hope of His calling, and what the riches of His inheritance is in the saints and what is the exceeding greatness of His power to us who believe according to the working of His mighty power."

About the Author

Beverly McBride is a virtuous woman of God who opens her mouth with wisdom and in her tongue is the law of kindness. She was born in Suffolk, Virginia and later on in her tender years as a child relocated with her parents to live in Hampton, Virginia where she successfully completed public schools and thereafter attended Virginia Commonwealth University studying Occupational Therapy and Psychology.

Beverly's motivation and skill for the love of writing has proven to be a God given gift utilized for the purpose of His glory. Inspired by the Holy Spirit, Beverly has been graced to share with The Body of Christ from the Word of God hidden treasures that have encouraged, esteemed, strengthened and blessed others.

Aside from the love of writing and during her quiet times alone with the Lord, she also enjoys singing and reading. Delighting in the "crown" of being a dedicated grandmother to her three precious granddaughters-Beverly's faithfulness, loyalty, and commitment shared with her family is witnessed to be inspiring, uplifting and most infectious.

Chapter 1. *P..* "*Practicing The Presence of God*"

"My presence shall go with you and I will give you rest."
Exodus 33: verse 14 [AMP]

In light of God's Word my aim is to show how you, the believer, can actually learn to practice being in the very presence of God.
Whether you realize it or not, practicing being in the presence of God is like being in the face of God.
You may be saying to yourself, "Sister Beverly, please explain to me how is that even possible?"

In response to your question if you would for just one moment, try to form in your mind a mental visual image of calling one of your dearest and closest friends on the telephone to extend a special invitation to meet you for dinner at one of the most exclusive restaurants in town.

This lavish five star restaurant you have chosen as a place to fellowship, known for its stupendous reputation without doubt has the means to surely soothe every fiber of your being as its ushers in a peace unlike any other can.
The excitement you hear transmitted from your friend's voice in accepting this special invitation both encourages and celebrates that fellowship is indeed pivotal in our established relationships shared with others.

Coming together in this fashion both parties are granted an opportunity to converse face to face and heart to heart by way of exchanging concepts and ideas, to minister Godly counsel one to another, to inspire, to eagerly encourage, and to join together in prayer for God's divine intervention.
These familiar types of communication skills once carefully cultivated will serve two extraordinary purposes.

First and foremost without doubt; it will eradicate the core to self-centeredness or better yet said, the "I Syndrome" which will allow each party to focus in on the other and secondly, it promotes a deeper level of mutual respect and sensitivity for one another.

This practical scenario is one of many ways by which a believer can use as a model to tap into being in the presence or in the *face* of God.

    Let's take a moment to reflect and direct our attention on Moses who accepted God's invitation to commune with Him, face to face.

In the book of Exodus chapter thirty three beginning at verses 7-10 we are told that whenever Moses would enter into the *tabernacle*, there would appear a cloudy pillar from heaven that descended in his midst while the LORD *talked* with Moses. As we read further along in verses 8-11 we are told that the LORD spoke with Moses *face* to *face* as a man naturally would speak and talk to his friend.

    You see, the face of God constitutes the *glory* of God, which is the supernatural or better yet one of the many attributes that personifies the true character of God!

When Moses entered into the *tabernacle*, the spirit of the LORD met him there. As he began to make daily contact with Him through verbal communication, Moses was then able to embrace God's *glory*.

As a result of his continual coming to being face to face, heart to heart, and soul to soul with God, Moses increased mightily in wisdom, knowledge, and power as a chosen leader to the children of Israel.

Through communing daily and spending quality time with God as he became saturated in His presence, something amazing happened!

After Moses's return back to his camp, the children of Israel both witnessed and saw the supernatural transference of God's glory that glistened on Moses's face!

> *You see, one of the greatest and dearest blessings that any believer can enjoy is being near to God.*

Your essential time spent alone with God is priceless and it yields His perspective on your life as you follow Him one step at a time. To hear God's voice you must seek him with all of your heart above all else; just as Moses did. He seized every opportunity that was presented to him by God as a privilege and an honor to talk with Him face to face.

Moses and God had developed such a mutual friendship with one another that God was able to trust and reveal to Moses His strategies in bringing the children of Israel out of captivity from the hands of Pharaoh.

In the book of Amos 3:7 [**AMP**] it is written that "surely the Lord God will do nothing without revealing His secret to His servants the prophets."

As a result to Moses's submission to God's plan, The Spirit of The Lord was able to move freely within him that gained access to satiate him with His heavenly Presence.

What greater delight or satisfaction could ever compare to this shared friendship between The Father and Moses!

God takes pleasure in your fellowship and is delighted to shine His glorious light on you as He did with Moses. Christ in You the hope of glory as quoted in Colossians chapter one and verse 27 is archetypal of this truth that God's spirit dwells on the inside of you!

The day that you and I believed, accepted and called on the name of the Lord Jesus to enter into our hearts, the "weight" (or the *glory*) of His Divine Nature was deposited within your inner man, causing you to become a new species that has never existed before!

His magnificence, splendor, holiness, rarity, loveliness, zeal, nobility, riches, authority, sovereignty, cleanliness, sobriety, solemnity, prosperity, wealth, health, anointing, honor and so very much more are merely some of the many outstanding attributes that we inherit and receive as He rubs them off on us from practicing being in the presence of God.

It has oftentimes been said that "Association brings about Assimilation."

This profound cliché has held its own title of truth for many generations.

In the natural realm, the same holds true of the child who holds high in esteem both parents as he follows their patterns by emulating and imitating their true character.

The more quality time that we spend in practicing God's presence, the more apt we are to walk like the Father, talk like the Father, act like the Father, and able to hear the Father's voice with clarity, which puts one in a position to become more consciously aware of Him and to become more cognizant of His presence at all times.

By keeping this objective in mind, let's focus in on two key component words that will be emphasized throughout this chapter and they are the words *"practice"* and the word *"presence."*

The first key component word mentioned that we will focus on is the word "practicing," which can be defined as the habitual, recurrent, frequent, repetitive method of an individual performing an activity and or skill consistently on a regular basis in order to obtain proficiency in carrying it out until it becomes "second nature."

In proving this definition to be true, let's take a walk into the Word of God and review how God operated in this very same principle.

According to the King James version of The Bible, we find in the book of Genesis chapter 1 beginning at verse 3 where God said: **"Let there be light: and there was light and immediately God saw the light. Then God called the light day, and the darkness He called night. God said let there be a firmament in the midst of the waters and God made the firmament and God called the firmament Heaven."**

We learn from this account in Genesis how God brought forth also the grass upon the earth, to every herb yielding seed after its own kind, to the gathering of the waters that God called the Seas to every living creature that moved from the fowls of the air to the fish in the sea to be fruitful and to multiply. God so wonderfully demonstrated here by Supreme Example that He not only executed His words to bring about life's existence; but by and through His words, He exercised His Divine Authority and Lordship by means of practicing His very own presence.

God repeatedly spoke these profound words of:

"Let there be....." until it became a natural habit for Him in calling forth those things to be as He released them from out of His mouth mixed with great faith.

Another glorious act that highlights the usage of God's word being exercised in practicing His very own Presence is referred to in this way:

"For He spake and it was done; He commanded, and it stood fast." Psalms 33:9 KJV

I like the way how the prophet Jeremiah extols God's greatness by acknowledging His creative power which was demonstrated in calling the heavens and the earth as we read in Jeremiah 32:17 KJV.

"Ah Lord GOD! Behold, thou hast made the heaven and the earth by thy great power and stretched out arm, and there is nothing too hard for thee."

With one single word by the breath of God's mouth, we continue to read that God made the structure of the heavens and its splendor by merely commanding them to be as He practiced His presence in the glory of Creation.
"By the word of the Lord were the heavens made and all the host of them by the breath of his mouth." Psalms 33:6

What do you believe will happen if a true believer would walk by faith and not by sight should he choose to operate in this same anointing as Jesus? Jesus uttered these words:

"Verily, verily, I say unto you, He that believeth on me, the works that I do *shall he do also; and greater works than these shall he do*; because I go unto my Father." John 14:12 [*Italicized for Emphasis*]

You may ask yourself, "How is this so?"
In the book of **John 14:16-17** Jesus gives us the answer with these words: **"And I will pray the Father, and he shall give you another Comforter, that he may abide with you forever. Even the Spirit of truth; whom the world cannot receive, because it seeth him not, neither knoweth him; but ye know him; for He dwelleth with you, and shall be in you."**

Jesus has made it quite clear to us that the living power of The Holy Spirit that dwells on the inside of every believer is the *empowering force* that enables and equips you and I to do *remarkable* exploits in His name.

In the second clause of this passage Jesus assures His people that He will intercede, fulfill and answer their prayers whether it be for themselves or on the behalf of others.

The true beauty of it all gives proof of His Divine Being and Omnipotence in what He has declared, He will most certainly perform!

Jesus said; **"I will do whatever you ask in My name, so that the Father may be glorified in the Son. You may ask Me for anything in My name, and I will do it."**
John 14:13-14 NIV

As Christian representatives we can operate in this same authority God has given to us on earth, yet it is not to say that our works will surpass God's power and majesty.
We, as believers must also add faith to ignite "God's spoken words," the main ingredient necessary for manifestation.

"Now faith is the substance of the things hoped for, the evidence of things not seen." Hebrews 11:1 KJV

As you begin to declare and meditate on God's written Word, allow His words to simmer, to saturate and to penetrate the very core of your heart (spirit) until it reaches a point of fervency, or better yet until it comes to a boiling point where total consumption overtakes the inner man (spirit) with what God's Word declares that you can have.
This intense method when executed is well suited for experiencing the manifested Promises of God's Word that never fails!
God summons every believer to be stirred up with hope and expectancy of believing His spoken Word to come to pass at its appointed time by simply "calling forth those things that be not as though it were." (See Romans 4:17.)
Virtually, every step to our *faith walk* in obedience to God places a believer in a position not only to *speak* God's Word; but to obtain success by possessing what he *desires* from the Word!

Understand this one important fact child of God, that His words are invigorating, masterful and commanding when you put your faith to work!

God's invention for the words that He speaks is never spoken in vain, nor does it fail to carry out His blueprint. His Word is sufficiently and adequately accompanied with power, life, and comfort as the scripture describes in the book of Isaiah 55:11.

> "So shall my word be that goeth forth out of my mouth; it shall not return unto me void, but it shall accomplish that which I please, and it shall prosper in the thing whereto I sent it."

So tell me, what are some of the promises from God's Word you have desired to come to pass in your life?
"Are you exercising the Word given to you and taking it to God in prayer?" If not, I beseech you to do so now.

Jesus, Himself said in **Matthew 11:29-30** these words: **"Take my yoke upon you, and learn of me, for I am meek and lowly in heart: and ye shall find rest unto your souls."**

Jesus tenderly exhorts every believer to look unto Him as being *The Example* by which we are to learn from in order to obtain true success in practicing His presence as He reveals Himself to us through His Spirit during our times of fellowship.

The guaranteed satisfaction of the believer who spends quality time with God and rests in His loving presence, is the one who will come to know and progressively experience all that He is!

Yet knowing this truth, there will be many that will abandon this great privilege due to fear and uncertainties by neglecting this opportunity of entering into His presence. Uncertainties that can easily rob one from deriving benefit of having a closer bond and a more intimate relationship with God have been those questions that some have entertained for decades.

One of the most rehearsed is the question of doubt that says, "What prerequisites are there that I must attain in order to actually qualify to witness His presence?"

First and most importantly, the only prerequisite that God requires is that we *believe in* Him and that we *believe on* Him! To answer your question regarding witnessing God's Presence, Paul tells us exactly how and the reason behind this mystical mindset to *thinking* that you must attain or perform some ritual in hopes to be in His Presence. Because of the finished works of Jesus, and what His blood fully accomplished on Calvary's Cross, Paul reminds you and I that we can both courageously and unreservedly approach Jesus and gain access to His tender loving Presence forever more free of charge!

(See Romans 5:2, Ephesians 2:18, 3:12 KJV)

So come quickly and Enter Into His Presence!

In support of this truth let us also carefully embrace God's written (Logos) Word that is found in John1:12 which guarantees this promise:

"But as many received him, to them He
gave *power* to become the sons of God
even to them that *believe* on His name."

So gird up your faith today and set your will to firmly grasp, *believe* and to *receive* the blessed right of being His child and instead of promoting doubt, fear and wrong thoughts that drain your faith from entering into His Presence, be daring, be strong, confident, and remain free from these plagues that so desperately tries to rob you of your privileges. It is now time to *draw near* to God!

*Understand this child of God, that your faith
has an innate ability to suppress and silence doubt
even in the most calamitous and grim situations.*

The Bible gives an excellent example to this type of stamina that was evident in the life of King Jehoshaphat.
He was a firm believer in God who in fact, demonstrated true courage as he faced his worst enemy in the battle against the Moabites and the Ammonites.

Let's take a look at his obedience in believing on the promise of God as recorded in II Chronicles 20:20 that is recorded in the Old Testament.

King Jehoshaphat was exhorted by God to affirm his faith by *trusting* God and to encourage his troops in the face of the enemy to do two significant things and through his obedience, The Lord showed the king and his troops His everlasting mercy and experienced victory that was celebrated with praise and solemn thanksgiving.
These two instructions that were carried out by the king is found in verse 20 which reads as follows:

> ...*believe* in the Lord your God, so shall ye
> be established; *believe* his prophets, so shall
> ye prosper."

Jehoshaphat's testament to us as believers proved that God is able to deliver our soul in peace from the battles that are sometimes against us and when we call upon Him in complete *trust*, He will heed to our voice and save us from all harm. King Jehoshaphat's secret in regaining victory as he threw himself on the everlasting mercies of God assured him that there was no need to cave in, give in or quit in this battle.

Despite the many challenges and adverse circumstances that encircled him, Jehoshaphat was fully convinced and consciously aware of God's Sovereign protection, as he faced the perilous odds that seemed to be against him.

Isn't it so amazing how rather than giving himself to worry, panic, and to pity with the odds that faced him, he was able to withstand the test by *trusting* in the Lord and wait patiently on His counsel. If we don't confer with God by submitting ourselves completely to Him, our end result will be undeniably powerless, ineffective, futile and at will unproductively unfruitful.

Yet, when we seek His advice and give ourselves to Him, we can expect to have a life that is most fulfilling, and to experience total peace and irrefutable victory in every situation at all times!

"Do you ever wonder if you are really *believing* and *trusting* God for what His Promises decrees you have obtained by the shed blood of Jesus?"

When you think about it, I want you to commune with the Holy Spirit by focusing on these next few words of hope that your heart might be encouraged the more as you grow in His grace to completely *trust* Him as Lord.

T…**Thinking** about God's Covenant you have with Him all of the time.   See Joshua 1:8 Isaiah 26:3

R…**Realizing** what Jesus' Shed Blood has done for you.   See Hebrews 9:22, 26

U…**Understanding** fully that God loves you without fail!   See Romans 5:8 I John 3:1

S… **Stay** focused on what God's Word has Promised you.   See Proverbs 30:5

T…**Thankfulness** expressed To The Father Continually!   See Philippians 4:8
                         See Ephesians 5:19

Thus far, we have talked about the two most significant types of pre-requisites which are *belief* and *trust*.

These two "spiritual twins" are instinctively important in tapping into the presence of God and should be your primary focus to having a more deeper and committed relationship with Him.

To Trust God is to know Him...
To Believe God is to accept Him!

That leaves us to the next question that many have pondered over in their relationship with The Lord in asking, "What is my role of responsibility to being in a committed relationship with God and what exactly is God's expectation of me?"

How many of us would agree that King David would be the perfect example to model after as we examine closely in the next few passages of how he pursued God's Presence and what was expected of him in this awesome relationship.

Let's see how God desires for you and I to minister to Him as we open our eyes to these life-changing truths.

This Psalm that King David records was used as a liturgy that tenderly introduces us how to provoke God's Presence and above all, to become more God-conscious.

In these passages King David also sheds light on how responsive God is to those who will diligently continue to aim, strive and seek His righteousness by following His Spirit.

Now then, let's get started and began to delve into the Word of God and embrace this truth that King David modeled for our learning found in **Psalms 4:3-5.**

The first step mentioned declares:

"But know that the Lord hath set apart him that is godly for himself." "The Lord will hear when I call unto him."

God is a God of divine order and the very first prerequisite we must be willing to practice is being consecrated and separated unto Him.

In the book of II Corinthians 6:17-18 The Bible says: "Wherefore come out from among them, and be ye separate says the Lord and touch not the unclean thing; and I will receive you and will be a Father unto you, and ye shall be my sons and daughters, says the Lord Almighty."

Learning to yield to God in this capacity enables one to benefit the optimum return of God's presence to be "meet for the Masters use, and prepared unto every good work."
(See II Timothy 2:21 KJV.)

The second step mentioned declares:
> **"To stand in awe.."**

To simply stand in awe of God means to acknowledge and to show reverential fear of who God is. As we look to the book of Revelation, the first chapter and verse ten we find where John speaks ..."I was in the spirit on the Lord's day and heard behind me a great voice as of a trumpet, and I turned to see the voice that spoke with me.... and when I saw him, I fell at his feet as dead."

The third step declares:
> **"Sin not...**

In Psalm 119:10-11 David so eloquently pledges his allegiance to God to become as a vessel of holiness by declaring: "With my whole heart I have sought thee,
O, let me not wander from thy commandments:
Thy word have I hid in my heart that I might not sin against thee."

The fourth step declares:
> **"To commune with your own heart**
> **upon your bed..."**

This passage of scripture simply encourages the believer to communicate intimately in an unrestricted and unrehearsed way with God in prayer.

King David said in Psalm 77:6 these tender words.
"I call to remembrance my song in the night: I commune with mine own heart: and my spirit made diligent search."
He sang songs of adoration and praise as he stood in acclamation of God's power until he sensed the very presence of God being near him.

The fifth step admonishes the believer to simply:
"Be still."

This phrase simply speaks as a command of being attentive and open to God's lead, and instructions that are given to the believer.

This step enables the believer to distinguish His voice when He speaks and to sharply discern proper judgment when given.
The book of Psalm 46:10 says it this way:
"Be still and know that I am God."

The sixth step directs the believer to:
"Offer the sacrifices of righteousness..."

This step suggests that Christians must take the initiative to present our lives and our bodies unto The Lord as our sacrificial and reasonable service unto Him.

As each of us yield our lives to The Lord in this way, we can expect to experience the security and mercy in our relationship with God in a much greater way.

The seventh and final step declares to:
"Put your trust in the Lord."

In response to Proverbs 3:5-6 we are charged to:
"Trust in the Lord with all your heart; and lean not unto your own understanding in all thy ways acknowledge Him, and He shall direct thy paths."

Trusting God with all of your being is the place where true worship gives birth to praise!

As we learn how to practice God's presence by releasing faith to trust HIM and thanking HIM for the finished works of Jesus, it is through these channels whereby we gain access to the pathways of living a victorious life!

This master key opens the path to being in the perfect will of God upon receiving all that He has given to us by basking in His presence during the sweet hour(s) of prayer.

…"In quietness and confidence shall be your strength..."
(See Isaiah 30:15.)

Once this step is mastered, it is then that our lives will become more governed and directed to follow Him on that solitary path that leads us by the calm, soothing and still waters.

The moment you begin to pursue God by putting these seven basic principles into practice you can expect to experience the tangible manifestation of the promise that truly "Glory and honor are in his presence, strength and gladness are in his place." (See I Chronicles 16:27 KJV.)

Now that we have discovered the meaning of the word "practice" and how it can benefit you, let's examine the word *"presence"* and discover how God releases the very essence of who He is to the believer while being in His very midst.

Being in the presence of God brings about the very nature of God.

Let's look at this simplistic equation that I have provided to help bring understanding of God's abiding Presence.

$$His\ Presence + His\ Nature = His\ Spirit.$$

To bring clarity to this statement come with me and let's begin to explore this Biblical truth as we look to the Word of God.

The Bible portrays heaven to be a place that is occupied with the glory of God's presence.

We are told that the angels of God stand in His Presence and act accordingly under His sovereign authority as He gives command. (See Luke 1:19.)

God's Presence is characterized and revealed to us in many forms.

For example, David sought the Lord's Presence in this fashion when he faced his enemy, Abimelech and he cried out to God as he ushered in His presence by saying:

"I sought the Lord, and he heard me, and delivered me from all my fears." Psalm 34:4

Ultimately, to experience God's Presence for any believer is the greatest blessing of all-and for those who share this bless-ed hope to His return will someday come to experience the glorious event of The Rapture, and see the shining of His face for all eternity. (See Psalm 67:1.)

I presented to you earlier the equation showing that the Presence of God constitutes His *Nature* that gives transcendent purity to His *Spirit*.

To simply describe His *Nature* is to understand that God is Supreme above all in every aspect of *goodness* and in Him, no evil dwells whatsoever! The Bible calls this goodness, *holiness*.

The very *nature* of God's character is holy and it is demonstrated from His love which explains why He can do no evil.

The word of God declares in I Peter 2:21-23:

"For even hereunto were ye called: because Christ also suffered for us, leaving us an example that ye should follow his steps: Who did no sin, neither was guile found in his mouth: who when he was reviled, reviled not again; when he suffered, he threatened not; but committed himself to him that judges righteously."

We who worship God must approach this last part of the equation in knowing both whose and "which temple ye are." God's very nature in essence is His Spirit and it is quite evident that all true worshippers who worship Him must approach Him with the part of us which is our *spirit*, in the *true temple* of God.   (See 1 Corinthians 6:19.)

"God is a spirit: and they that worship him must worship him in spirit and in truth."   John 4:24

King David acknowledged God's presence as being a Spirit by saying; "Whither shall I go from thy spirit? Or whither shall I flee from thy presence?"   Psalm 139:7

To share more revelation on this insight let's continue reading and take careful study of several scriptures to support these three Divine attributes of the essence of His Presence.

The Bible reminds us in the book of Genesis 1: verse 2 that while the earth was being formed, the Spirit of God was present-giving life to that which was once not in existence.

"And the earth was without form and void;
and darkness was upon the face of the deep
and the *spirit* of God (Presence) moved upon
the face of the waters."

Just as God's Spirit moved upon the face of the waters, He too desires to move freely in and through you to demonstrate His glory here on the earth in these last days as a sign and as a wonder in this dark world.

By allowing Him this opportunity, it correspondingly reveals and expands the aspects to the Spirit of God's character represented in you which is manifested in the peaceable fruits of His Divine Nature.

As I meditated on this thought, it was no sooner that I had begun to inquire of the Lord by asking Him to reveal to me, "What are some of the ingredients that I should be looking for in the peaceable fruits of His Divine nature?" Days seemed to have passed by me so quickly as I eagerly anticipated in hearing God's voice to answer this pending question. Constantly, as I sat in His presence, and calmly remained quiet in speech, God directed me to the book of Galatians, the secret place where hidden treasure had been tucked away, concealed and preserved for such a time as this for me to find.

God's revelation shown to me concerning the fruit of His Divine Nature is analogous to taking (orally) a daily natural supplemental vitamin to build up our immunity system to eliminate deficiencies that sometimes takes place in our human bodies. You see, the fruit of God's spirit which Paul describes in the book of Galatians 5:22-23 works similarly in the very same manner.

"But the fruit of the Spirit (of God) is love, joy, peace, longsuffering, gentleness, goodness, faith, meekness, temperance against such there is no law."

This revelation that God showed me concerning the fruit of His Spirit will certainly make you more cognizant of His glorious presence and without fail equip you for the journey throughout each passing day!

When a true believer continually abides in God's Presence and relies on Him to supply their every need it is analogous to the athlete who consistently trains properly by implementing taking vitamins on a daily basis.

This type of discipline that is exercised will produce strength in times of weakness and spiritually keep them buoyant during those tough times of combat against the tempter.

Remaining conscious of God's presence as you go throughout the day guarantee's His sure protection along the way. God's daily dosage prescribed for the believer will always cause you to triumph in every situation and circumstance that confronts you!

I want you to take a close look at what you, *the believer* can expect from God by walking in the spirit.

When the fruit of God's love is taken it helps to shield against the spirit of hate, when joy is taken it helps to shield against the spirit of depression, longsuffering when taken helps to fight against impatience, gentleness when taken helps to fight against ill will, goodness when taken it helps to shield against hatred and strife, faith when taken it helps to shield against fear and doubt, meekness when taken it helps to shield against haughtiness, pride and arrogance, and lastly when temperance is taken it helps to shield against the attitude of self-indulgence.

What do you think would happen to the believer that chooses not to develop this type of attitude?

The answer to this question is quite apparent.

When we choose not to walk in the fruit of God's spirit it is then that our lives take on an entirely different direction than what God wills.

The reciprocal of choosing the conscious decision to step away from operating in the fruit of the Spirit will lead you astray by enticing one to walk in the dictates of your flesh.

Here are some prime examples of the believer that does not adhere to taking the daily dosage of God's Divine Spirit that is spoken of in Galatians 5:19-21 KJV.

"Now the works of the flesh are manifest such as these: Adultery, fornication, uncleanness, lasciviousness, idolatry, witchcraft, hatred, variance, emulations, wrath, strife, seditions, heresies, envying's, murders, drunkenness, reveling, and such like…."

"What peaceable fruits of God's spirit are being escorted into your house of prayer?"

Perhaps, it is the spirit of joy that overrides despondency and depression in your life-and if so David was an excellent example of choosing joy to be his defender.

We read in the book of Psalm where King David found joy even in the midst of his trials as he escaped to find solace into the Holy of Holies as he ran to enter the secret place of the Most High God.

His direct and candid communication with God in prayer is oftentimes expressed melodiously with words of joy.

This joy that is taken as the fruit of the Spirit most certainly served David as being a weapon of warfare that positively defeated his depression, deep sadness and sorrow.

David found comfort in God and declared:

> "Thou wilt show me the path of life:
> in thy presence is fullness of joy; at thy right
> hand there are pleasures for ever more."
>
> Psalm 16:11

So receive these gifts of God, and walk in the operation of His power and make a daily profession of them that you are led and influenced by The Holy Spirit to be fruitful in every good work. Amen.

For the remaining part of this chapter, I have purposely added other supplemental Biblical accounts that are purposed solely to highlight the significance of God's Spirit (Presence) in all of Creation.

I would like for us to focus on ten words spoken out of the mouth of God in Genesis 1:26 that highlights the sculpturing and fashioning of *The Creation of Man* and it reads:

> "… and God said, Let us make man in our image after our likeness…"

When God created man, He created him in excellence to be perfectly flawless, beautiful, authoritative, and good. Man was not created by some mystical accident, or from a scientific experiment or by chance.

God conceived Man as a thought, nurtured the thought, and released the thought with faith-filled words and by His Spirit, He expertly designed Man in the very graphic resemblance of Himself by His unsurpassed wisdom and prodigious power.

Imagine this- that the God of the Universe loved you and I so much that His desire was to fashion, form, shape, fill, mold, and sculpture us in the very graphic representation of Himself. What a privilege and honor it is to represent Him in the earth as His sons and daughters! Hallelujah!

With much thought and meticulous planning in the Creation of Man, God in His manifold wisdom took and transported His "Zoe" life directly into the physical nature of Man causing him to have existence on the earth.

> "And the LORD God formed man of the dust of the ground, and breathed into his nostrils the breath of life; and man became a living soul." Genesis 2:7

A new species was now formed in the presence of God that flowed freely into the three realms of Adam's existence which affected his spirit, soul and his physical body.

Another Bible revelation that depicts God's presence is also found in Genesis 3:8 that acknowledges:
"And they (Adam and Eve) heard the voice of the Lord God walking in the garden in the cool of the day and Adam and his wife hid themselves from the presence of the Lord amongst the tree of the garden."
It is here where we find the strategic place where God walked: *In the garden* which was the primary residence of Adam and Eve.

God's presence on that particular day phenomenally impacted their lives in such a way that confidently assured them that HE was both their shield and armor.
This strong attachment that Adam and Eve had grown accustomed to sharing with God escalated and elevated them in deeper levels to having a more solid, grounded and most meaningful union in their relationship!
God is so mindful and considerate of us that He chooses to visit us even during times when we least expect Him.
Psalm 8:4 carefully announces:
 "What is man that thou art mindful of him? and the sons of man that thou visit him?"

The angels of God marveled and spoke among themselves as they carefully observed the creation of man as God fashioned him. They gazed and looked intently from the heavens and witnessed how God both walked and talked with him.

They also took careful watch of the close fellowship that was formed and shared between the two. Can you imagine what the angels must whisper to one another as you and I gather together in unison with God, The Father during our times of prayer?

I am confident to say that when we do enter into the Holy of Holies, and enter into the courts of our God, we have a cloud of witnesses accompanying us by an heavenly host of angels, strategically put in place to hearken to our voice-given to God's word.

"How does God *respond* and *react* to our continual coming into His presence?"

The answers given to that question is found in a few scripture references that I have chosen specifically that are quoted below for our learning.

Isn't it wonderful to know that we have a Heavenly Father who regards us to be His best friends and One who takes pleasure to walk in our midst and at will, to be actively involved in every intricate part of our lives?

One of many supporting scriptures that upholds this truth is found in Matthew 18:20 when Jesus declared unto the disciples:

> **"For where two or three are gathered together in my name there am I in the midst of them."**

If you are already living in this truth, this is good news!

One of God's desire is that you choose to include and share with Him practically everything that goes on in your life. He wants to play a big role in ways that concerns your agendas, your business affairs, in the raising and nurturing of your children, in your marriage, and even those seen and unseen potential challenges you may be experiencing on your job and other activities that I may not have mentioned.

I believe if every Christian will take the time to fully understand and encompass this truth, they will discover more and more about God and how He longs to live in fellowship with them on a continual basis.

Another account that bears witness as to how Jesus *responds* and *reacts* to those who seek His Presence, is characterized by this "cheerful greeting" as He welcomed the disciples after having been resurrected and raised from the dead.

> **"And as they went, behold, Jesus met them and said, Hail (greetings)! And they went up to Him and clasped His feet and worshipped Him."**
> **Matthew 28:9 [AMP]**

Before Jesus was crucified and ascended up to Heaven, He carefully explained in conversations held with the disciples that on the third day, He will rise and see them again.

Jesus said; **"He is not the God of the dead, but the God of the living."** **(See Mark 12:27)**

"What kind of thoughts do you imagine the disciples had when they saw Jesus on that particular day and heard His cheerful greeting that was directed towards them?"

On the flip side of this question, I can imagine how it must have felt for Jesus. In my past experiences over the years as a former legal secretary, meeting and greeting new clients regularly had become my passion.

There were many times throughout the course of my days when I thrived off of every opportunity that presented itself to welcome and greet the company's clientele in such a manner that vibrated joy, enthusiasm, delightfulness and excitement.

As a result, many of the clients were just as excited as I was to have been treated in a manner that gave them a feeling to know that they mattered and most importantly, of being respected and shown appreciation for their business.

The clients seemed to have been thrilled by the calming of my voice and inspired by the joy that was on my face.

I can only imagine how the chosen disciples must have felt when Jesus met with them face to face once more.

Jesus rejoices over you and welcomes you with open arms every time you come to inquire and commune with Him.

You are His greatest delight and His innermost joy!

In this next passage of Scripture, we can see clearly how Jesus used another method when He acknowledged Peter's presence at a time when he needed assurance and hope.

I want you to hear with your heart these calm, consoling, and reassuring words that Jesus spoke to Peter as we turn our attention over to the gospel of **Matthew 14:25-29.**

"And in the fourth watch of the night Jesus went unto them, walking on the sea. And when the disciples saw him walking on the sea, they were troubled saying, It is a spirit; and they cried out for fear. But straightway Jesus spake unto them, saying, *Be of good cheer; it is I; be not afraid* and Peter answered Him and said, Lord if it be thou, bid me come unto thee on the waters and He said, *Come.* And when Peter was come down out of the ship, he walked on the water to go to Jesus."   [*Italicized for Emphasis*]

Tell me, what special greeting do you recall that God welcomed you with that just brought complete joy and contentment to your heart during your most recent time spent alone with Him?

Don't be surprised when the next time you are talking with The Father that He calls out to you by name, He is our Father and He knows us all by our names! Hallelujah.

Be fully aware in understanding that His continual, permanent and enduring Presence is the solid affirmation which gives true meaning to one of His many names, Emanuel- "God with us." Remember, God is with You!

Interestingly enough, there is still yet more for us to learn about practicing being in the Presence of God.
Now follow me very closely as we begin to re-focus on how a believer can approach God as he enters into His courts.
I want you to go back with me to the very beginning of this chapter when you were asked to envision yourself reconnecting with an old friend by way of inviting them out for dinner.
As you fix your eyes once again at this depiction, I want you to begin first by visualizing Jesus in a new light, by seeing Him as being your Best Friend!

When I reflect on those who are dearest to me, I think about those friends who I can call on the phone to talk to when I need someone to listen. They are the first people I think of when something most important takes place in my life, and when I need a shoulder to cry on I can always count on them to encourage me and even make me laugh.
They are the kind of friends who fully understand everything about me, who I am, what my likes and dislikes are; and one thing is for certain that I can always depend on-and that is knowing they always have my best interest at heart!
Having best friends means all different things to many people.
Some even believe that you can have only one or three best friends at the most.

Others assert having best friends to be those that typically meet characteristics that are generally similar to their personality traits.

But whatever the reason may be, Jesus desires to be your Best Friend Forever and Always regardless of one's peculiarities.

Let's discover together how you can attain this newly found friendship that God wants to have with you!

One of many ways by which God has made provisions for a believer to acquire entrance into His presence by way of cultivating a true friendship with Him, is through the personal invitation that He extends directly to you.
By accepting this invitation, it will require a leap of child-like faith to begin the process.

"Can you think of any better way to being invited to spend time with The God of the Universe?"
What can surpass such an invitation as this?

The Scripture reminds us that we must first seek God and by doing so, the end result to this motion taken gives promise that He will be found as stated in the book of I Chronicles 28:9 KJV.

"....If thou seek him, he will be found of thee..."

The Bible also makes mention as to how God extends open invitations to those who recognize their need for a Savior in Revelation 3:20 KJV.
Jesus's humble and gentle approach that He extends by way of invitation to reach and to relate to Man speaks to us in this melodic way.

"Behold, I stand at the door, and knock: if any man hear my voice and open the door, I will come in to him and will sup with him, and he with me."

So then, dear friends, the door of God's heart has now been opened and no longer fastened.
How many times has He has knocked and tapped at the door of your heart?
Will you neglect His invitation of friendship that has been offered?
Do you realize how much satisfaction it brings to God for you to open up your heart to Him?

The patience of Christ and His tender mercies awaits your admission!

Those of us who choose to open our hearts to Him shall indeed enjoy His sweet presence.
    The passage also tells us that Christ will sup with those who accept His invitation which indicates to us that there is some type of a feast that has been prepared to celebrate this new friendship. We have taken a peek at God's spiritual perspective of His invitation offered to us, now let's take a moment to search how we can draw God into our presence.

Imagine this if you will, for every special occasion and major event that takes place in our lives that is worthy of recognition and praise, we as creatures of habit oftentimes deem it as necessary to share our joy with close friends and family by planning events of celebration.

If you can identify with this scenario more than likely, the very first task at hand to prepare for this event would be to notify your guests by mailing out the invitations in a timely manner.
These invitations would of course include the specific reason for the invite, the designated time the event would begin and end, the date of the event, the strategic location of the function and last but not least, a response card to RSVP.

When a believer set aside the time to cordially extend to God an invitation such as this, then certainly without a doubt He graciously accepts and enters into your presence bringing with Him in full measure the abundance of His love and joy in the complete essence of His Divine Being!

In accordance to Isaiah 55:6 it admonishes us in this way:
> "Seek, inquire for, and require the Lord while He may be found [claiming Him by necessity and by right]; call upon Him while He is near." **[AMP]**

Many examples are given to us in God's Word whereby men and women who sought to encounter His sweet presence reports to their hearers that when they entered into the presence of the Lord, it transcended boundaries almost impossible to describe.

Let's take a closer look at some of those who sought God with all of their hearts and as a result found themselves delighting in His presence.
Job, for example was a devout man who even in the times of great defeat, despair, calamity and great loss sought The Lord and in His presence, he found great solace and peace. In the book of Job 5:8-9 KJV Job declared:
> "I will seek unto God, and unto God will I commit my cause: which doeth great things unsearchable and marvelous things without number."

The psalmist used this heart-felt approach as a direct way to reach out to God in his times of despair and sorrow that has been recorded in the book of Psalm 17:1-2.
> "Hear the upright, O Lord attend unto my cry, give ear unto my prayer, that goes not out of unfeigned lips." Let my sentence come forth from thy presence;
> Let my sentence come forth from thy presence;
> let your eyes behold the things that are equal."

In reading this passage we can sense the longing of the psalmist plea as he draws near in faith to knowing that God hears him.

In spite of David and his many sins committed, he was sincerely repentant and sought after God with passion through fervent expressions in his prayers.

David prayed to the Lord:

"Create in me a pure (clean) heart, O God, and renew a steadfast spirit within me. Do not cast me from your presence or take your Holy Spirit from me."

Psalm 51:10-11 **NIV**

Much has been written and spoken about David in his heart-felt approach to God in the Old Testament as well as in the New Testament.

We most certainly can garner insight and learn many lessons from his relationship with The Lord.

By his example, we can learn how essential that it is for a believer to cling closely to God and thus, choose to make time alone with Him-your top priority.

David demonstrated by showing us that when we come together in the presence of God, we must not only pray and sing praise unto Him, but that we also must be; transparent, humble, trusting, reverent, obedient, and repentant towards Him. These words all describe the heart of David as they are rehearsed and seen in his very own writings throughout the Bible.

"How would you describe your frailties, blunders, and weaknesses to God?" "Would you be honest to confess your sins and humble yourself before God, who is the Only One that can forgive of sin as David's life has taught us?"

David's life is not one that should be judged based solely on his failures, but rather on the tenderness of his soul that touched and moved the heart of God!

"It is not so much what the nature of sin can bring in our lives, but it is primarily what one does about those failings when they are faced and confronted with having the fortitude to acknowledge them openly with honesty and genuineness."

The re-assuring factor to remember Child of God, is that God is a God of compassion and forgiveness who seeks to find and to restore those who have lost their way by bringing them back into His loving care.

Jesus promises those who will come to Him to give them what no one else could ever give-rest from the stress and burdens of sin, and a promise to soothe every sorrow which easily weighs on every individual's soul.

(See Matthew 11:28.)

So come quickly and enter into His rest-the invitation is at hand!

Other questions that sometimes remain dormant in the mind of many believers who are in search of the Lord's presence could very well be this suppressed internal thought, "What shall I bring when I come to seek God's face as I enter in to pray?" and lastly, "What can I expect to receive as an empowerment in my life as I spend time in His presence during prayer?"

First and most importantly, always be assured that in the believer's place of worship, God's presence is always revealed by signs and wonders that follow.

Thus, in spite of all eventualities a believer's confidence must lie in the fact that whether in times of suffering, heartache, or great joy or sorrow he/she must trust that the presence of God is available and that God's nearness is always present!

I like what Psalm 73:28 **[AMP]** has to say:

"But it is good for me to draw near to God;
I have put my trust in the Lord God and made
Him my refuge, that I may tell of all your works."

God wholeheartedly welcomes those who longs for Him by receiving and accepting heart felt sacrifices of praises presented unto Him as the scripture reminds us in Psalm 22:3 **[AMP]** that reads: *[Italicized for Emphasis]*
> "But you are holy, O You Who dwell in the Holy place where the *praises* of Israel are offered."

The Bible excitedly compels us to come and sing joy unto The Lord with a shout out to Him in jubilant celebration! According to the book of Psalm 95:1-2 it declares:
> "O, come let us sing unto the Lord: let us make a joyful noise to the rock of our salvation. Let us come before his presence with thanksgiving and make a joyful noise unto him with psalms."

Let's examine a specific time in Bible history of Jesus' birth to gain insight from what the wise men actually brought with them when they encountered Jesus' presence for the very first time.

According to Matthew's Gospel chapter two beginning at verse 11 we encounter the visit of the wise men and discover how they came, what they brought, and what expectation they all had when they came into the presence of the newborn King!

The scripture tells us in verse 11… **"And when they were come into the house, they saw the young child with Mary his mother, and fell down, and worshipped him: and when they had opened their treasures, they presented unto him gifts; gold, and frankincense, and myrrh."**

You see beloved, *"worship"* is another essential prayer tool that we as believers have been given as an expression of our celebrated love for the Father.

The wise men keenly felt the glorious presence of the newborn King and experienced God's anointing that surrounded him where they stood next to Joseph, Mary and baby Jesus.

Let's take a look at how God so tenderly admonishes us to come into His Presence.

The Psalmist so eloquently expresses his deep longing to be in the courts of the Lord in Psalm 95:6 by saying:

> **"O come, let us worship and bow down:**
> **let us kneel before the Lord our maker."**

We are to come into the presence of God with the joy of singing, making melody in our hearts with thanksgiving, worshiping and bowing down at the feet of our God, just as the wise men did that serves as an example to the Body of Christ!

Psalm 100:4 is one of the most notoriously known and beautiful prayer psalms that vividly guides and instructs the true believer as to how we are to enter into God's presence and the gifts of praise that should follow.

> "Enter in his gates with thanksgiving and into
> his courts with praise. Be thankful unto him
> and bless his name." Serve the Lord with
> gladness: and come before his presence with
> singing." Psalms 100:2

As you and I enter into the secret place of the most High God, the mentioning of giving thanks unto Him with a grateful heart purposefully gives room to having a greater revelation of who Jesus really is. This simple expression in giving thanks to God allows Him to participate in the life of a believer by proving and demonstrating His great love and immeasurable grace that He has for them!

The next concern we will need to address that many have searched for an answer to for decades is the question that asks, "What is it that I, the believer can expect to find from God by ushering in His presence during my prayer time?"

The answer to that question is found in the book of Psalm 96:6 [*Italicized for Emphasis*] and it reads:

"*Honor* and *majesty* are before him: *Strength* and *beauty* are in his sanctuary. Give unto the Lord; O ye kindred of the people give unto the Lord glory and strength. Give unto the Lord the glory due unto his name: bring an offering and come into his courts." "O worship the Lord in the beauty of holiness: fear before him, all the earth."

> *"Glory, honor, majesty, strength, beauty and holiness are the essential benefits derived from being in the presence of God."*

God unveils to us His heart as a loving Father while at the same time He shows us His sovereignty as Lord and King! The time has come for the Body of Christ to intimately become more acquainted with God's presence and to walk in the fullness of His glory.

"What on earth do you mean by that Sister Beverly?"

As we gravitate towards walking in His glory it should be evident, undeniable, obvious and plain for others to see as they witness His face (glory of His countenance) that shines brilliantly upon you!

In days of old holy men and women who walked with God, experienced what it was like to be in the presence of God and encountered His *glory*.

This *glory* appeared oftentimes and was recorded as being like a mighty rushing wind, while on other occasions it was described as a blazing fire that came down from heaven as well as likened unto a soft, misty, glowing cloud that hovered upon His people.

The very same God today is more than ready to show you that He is your abiding strength, your shield and your glory!

God earnestly desires for His glorious presence that abides in and thru you to take residence in your home, on the job, in the mall, in the barber shop, and even at your child's school.

Wherever you are willing to take Him, God is ever ready to go before you to assist and to make His presence boldly known.

I challenge you at this very moment to begin implementing by putting to practice these valuable lessons we have learned thus far in your fellowship with God.

These practical principles have been proven to benefit a believer when applied on a consistent basis.

So make haste in getting to your secret dwelling place of worship and began to construct your house of prayer, praise and worship today!

For in this secret place Jesus awaits to meet you there, and everything that you will need to build this foundation of prayer will be furnished and supplied by Him Alone, El-Shaddai.

"Now set your hearts and your soul to seek the Lord your God, Arise therefore and build ye the sanctuary."
I Chronicles 22:19 KJV

"Seek the Lord and his strength seek his face continually."
I Chronicles 16:11 KJV

Chapter 2. R.. "Reaching Towards Heaven"

*"I sought the Lord and he heard me and delivered me
from all my fears."*
Psalm 34: verse 4

In this particular chapter we will learn how to effectively communicate with God by touching and moving His very hand during the sweet melodies of prayer.
Once we discover the keys as to how this is done you will find it to be the most valuable, beneficial and priceless treasure beyond measure!
So let's get ready and begin to reach the higher heights in this splendid dimension of reaching God in heaven!

As proof of having any good relationship between two or more parties one must first learn how to identify, communicate and learn how to establish harmony with one another. Once these three essentials are cultivated it then yields the peaceable fruits for a successful and wholesome relationship.
It is my intent to help you understand that it is God's heart desire to be able to relate and reach you as much as your heart desire is to relate and reach Him.

In light of God's Word that is found in the book of II Chronicles 7:14 and verse 16 it beautifully depicts God's heart and how He desires for you and I to come unto Him. God's Word given instructs every believer on how to identify with Him, to communicate with Him heart to heart, and lastly how you and I can successfully establish a harmonious relationship with Him.

Now take a look for just one moment at this passage of scripture very closely as it gives a set of four conditions that these people are exhorted to do. Notice very carefully that if the four conditions are carried out there are three Promises that are outlined in this scripture which tells us that God will confer on them blessings.

I love how God responded to Solomon's request concerning the various provisions He set in order for Israel when they sinned against Him in this passage.

So, at this time let us come together and dissect each verse to gain understanding of what God's desire is for every believer to obtain. [*Italicized for Emphasis*]

Let's get started!

"If my people who are called by my name, shall humble themselves, and pray and seek my face, and turn from their wicked ways, *then will I hear from heaven*, and will *forgive their sin,* and will *heal their land*…for now have I chosen and sanctified this house, that My name may be there forever; and mine eyes and mine heart shall be there perpetually."

*If my people who are called by my name

There are two specific concepts that are key factors in this covenant relationship shared between God and Israel that we must understand…(1)Israel belonged to God; and (2) God's people that had sinned against Him were admonished first and foremost to confess, admit and to acknowledge this and thereby reverently humbly submit to God's Divine Authority.

*Pray and seek my face

The children of Israel are commanded to pray to God, and to animatedly seek, go after and to pursue God with all of their heart with a sense of knowing that they were admitted into His holy Presence.

*Turn from their wicked ways

Godly sorrow works repentance and by this action taken He will hear their prayers.

*Hear from heaven… Forgive their sin…Heal their land

When the children of Israel turned from their sinful ways God's ear was attentive to them whereby He was able to be *reached*, God showed them mercy by forgiving them and blessed their land immensely as He eagerly restored back to them their health, and amazingly their right standing, their good welfare and most importantly their hope.

What is this passage saying to you? I think this scripture is very explicit in explaining to the believer how we can better reach and be pleasing to God for reasons given below.

It is imperative that we should first begin this process by looking inwardly at ourselves and secondly, to show fortitude by way of confessing and to admit unreservedly to God when we have missed the mark and have turned our backs on Him. Thereby, as we humbly submit in reverent fear to HIS Almighty power and above all to HIS Divine Authority, repentance is granted and by having this this kind of attitude it quickly restores and bring us back in harmonious communion with The Father.

As Christians, we must all be committed to live a life that will bring unadulterated glory to The Father-and by doing so, we can expect to experience more of His Presence and witness such an torrent of The Holy Spirit regularly in our everyday lives.

The very proof to the *fruit of our repentance* becomes evident when we comply by taking heed to do the will of the Father with the aid of the Holy Spirit.

The fruit of our repentance obviously implies that there is a process which involves a lifelong adaptation to adhering in aligning our attitudes, behavior, mindsets and heart towards God and His precepts. Bearing this kind of fruit indicates to us that repentance is a gift that only God can grant to Man because of His grace.

This is key as to how God is able to draw and compel us and change our hearts towards Him.

Because of God's tender mercies and longsuffering we are wholeheartedly indebted to Him. God's kindness leads the believer not only to repentance but it opens the chambers of his heart to become more pliable as he initiates to communicate in regards to *reaching* and *relating* to God in a more meaningful way!

God's master design for man to be able to relate and reach Him has been the scope of Jesus's entire ministry-by engaging to bring Man away from his sins to repent and *turn* to Him.
When we do this, we accept His gift, and the connection that we have with Christ.

God's Master design for us all is recognizably amazing!
Take a good look at yourself.. YOU are an amazing masterpiece
from the fruit and the works of His Hands!

So get on board and come confidently before the throne of God, ask Him to help you yield your body and mind in complete subjection under His will as you place them in His hands and He will do great and mighty things to direct your course.

Rejoice and be glad Beloved of God, His Word expresses so affectionately these profound words as recorded in Jeremiah 33:3 [**AMP**]

> "Call to Me and I will answer you and show you great and mighty things, fenced in and hidden, which you do not know [do not distinguish and recognize, have knowledge of and understand]."

By guarding this promise in your mind, let's move forward and talk about how you can progressively come to develop that effectual communication with God as you begin to moderately reach and relate to Him in your very own personal way.

One of my thoughts to developing a more purposeful and secure "*God Kingdom relationship*" as I choose to describe, would be the daily practice of continually seeking His face with a mindset that focuses your attention that is entirely exclusively on Him.

As your time increases being in His Presence- you will soon discover that your journey is the predestined pathway, leading you closer to God that is the most effective way into gaining ultimately a much more consecrated and intimate "communion" with The Father. Think about that last statement that was made for one minute, that mentions our communion with The Father. Remember in the book of Genesis when God said,
"Let us make man in our own image," this was in fact the original purpose of God's success in His kingdom relationship with man.

God created Man with the purpose to have fellowship and to share all of His spiritual and earthly possessions with His family as He does with you!

As God's intimate Presence was with Adam, so is His Presence with *you* right now in every step you take-in every adventure and in every detour of your paths-He longs to "wrap" *you* in His everlasting Love at all times-no matter what turns *you* take. He is the only One who knows everything there is to know about *you*, and desires to be *your* Helper!

Through the aid of the Holy Spirit, He knows the deep secrets to the simplicities and intimacies of your entire being-(mind, heart and spirit) as no other person can. So let your guards down by gaining knowledge to simply trust Him in your *God Kingdom relationships*!

Learning to achieve this simple practice I believe, will help you to maintain a promising friendship that yields God's all-encompassing companionship, peace, protection, salvation, blessings, joy, love, wisdom, the ever present closeness to God and the abundance of His goodness.
Glory to God!

As you sit quietly reading this chapter my prayer for you is that you will experience *God's Glory* over your entire being and that you will remain close to Him and focus your thoughts on His love for you.

I pray that you will choose to "weave" these virtuous qualities into your life by practicing diligence and adding discipline to remain on course-that supernaturally launches you on your way towards *reaching* and *relating* to the Lord, your God.

I also believe, Beloved that there are other attractive qualities you can engender and incorporate in your personal *"God Kingdom relationship"* that can indeed promote and produce a harmonious, long-lasting, abiding and holy relationship with The Father.

Now then, let's look to see what are some of the other attractive qualities you can engender into your very own new *"God kingdom relationship"* as it relates to you getting to know Him!

The first condition that involves you getting to know God in a more personal way begins by making a decision of quality to accept the truth of His written Word, that declares Jesus is the Son of the Living God, and that He is the only sacrifice and offering accepted for our sins past, present and future. (See John 1:1-14 and Hebrews 10:14.)

Ultimately by choosing to make Jesus as Lord, the believer is gradually transformed and henceforth re-created into the image God originally intended for him to be.

This process of spiritual growth and maturity that takes place by bringing Him your sacrifice of time and trusting God to accomplish His finest and best work in you, is by far one of the most significant keys to *relating* to God and getting to know Him intimately.

God delights and takes pleasure when you come into His Presence to inquire of Him.

Devoting and sacrificing time to develop this type of intimacy requires the practice of making Him priority over and above all else.

The benefits that are reaped from your very own personal *God Kingdom relationship* is unreservedly priceless and symbolizes a testimony of God's unfailing Love.

When a true believer is determined to live his life under the direction of The Holy Spirit in this way, God's power can flow at will to meet every need by supplying and ministering aid with resources in areas of your life that will never run dry. You see Beloved, when God is considered as your highest priority and closest confidant a divine connection between those two hearts now become as One! This is the basis of a holy courtship that God designed for you before the foundation of the world. Now grip on to God's loving hands so tightly and walk with Him as He carries you across the threshold of grace, mercy and love.

Now arise, give God your hand and let the holy courtship begin!

This holy courtship between the Body of Christ and God, reminds me of the Walt Disney's first animated feature film during the 1930's and 1950's of *Beauty and the Beast.*
This was a story that focused on the relationship between the Beast who was magically cursed by an enchantress and is transformed into a unattractive, monstrous looking creature in sentence for his coarse and egotistical behavior-because the filling of his empty heart was void of the emotion "*to love.*"
The curse of the spell could only be broken when he learns how to love in hopes that love would be reciprocated by the young fair woman who was held captive against her own will in his castle.

However, if the Beast was not successful in learning how to love and to become loveable, he would remain under this dreadful curse as being animalistic, cynical and primitive without having a kind side to his nature for the rest of his life.
Very briefly, I wanted to share this story in effort to show how our relationship with God could have resulted if it had not been for His grace, love, favor and mercy that has been freely extended to you and I.

Without a shadow of doubt to our limited imagination, we would be a human race of victims trapped and snared under Satan's curse and denied the free gift of salvation's privilege of having the sheer blessedness of a Kingdom relationship with God!

I want you to see yourself prior to giving your life to Jesus as you read these next few paragraphs and afterwards if I may kindly suggest, began to worship Jesus, who is The Way, The Truth and The Life that rescued you and I with His unconditional Love-The Almighty God who rejoices over us with great joy. Hallelujah! (See Zephaniah 3:17.) "Who would you say represents Beauty better than anyone else ever could?" The answer to this question without doubt is **no one** greater than our God and His name is *Jesus*!

Tell me, "Who does the Beast remind you of?"

As you catch a glimpse of your former life of carnality-enjoying the pleasures of sin, you and I were in essence similar in nature to the Beast.

Our frail, shattered and empty lives without a covenant with God would have left us with this ugly exterior and trapped in hopelessness for a life of eternity.

The moral behind this endearing short story holds many truths that we all can learn by.

Notice in this story that the Beast never knew what true love was or even how to love until Beauty met him face to face.

Through Beauty's compassion, patience and courage that was shown to this terrible Beast expressed by this fair woman, he began to slowly receive and discover within the depths of his heart how to love and was amazed to learn that even while at his worst state of being he could *be loved*.

Thank God for His only begotten Son, Jesus and His shed blood that HE died an "open death" on the cross to prove HIS GREAT LOVE for us that had the power to deliver and set us-the captives free!

What a joyful and triumphant day it was when you and I received salvation to the saving of our souls-our spirit was regenerated and made anew at the very moment upon Jesus' entrance into our hearts.

The Bible paints a similar imagery of this occasion as being analogous to the regal celebration in the like fashion as a marriage ceremony between a bride and her groom.

This profound and most jubilant ceremony of the *joining together with God's spirit*-ignited with yours now gives birth to holy impartation which provides comfort, everlasting joy, security, provision and love in its most inevitable and purest form!

By keeping this in mind, we will now turn our attention to the second attractive quality that I believe is fundamentally proper as it relates to building a strong and honorable *God kingdom relationship*.

First and far most, it is expedient for every believer who genuinely desires to honor God respectfully to possess an attitude of *patience and submission, by waiting on God expectantly*.

If you are too anxious about any or everything that takes precedence over God's plan for your life-the end result will be to magnify your natural ability (self-glorification) as opposed to deriving the empowerment of His supernatural ability being manifested on your behalf.

Practicing to wait on God is a glorious benefit that keeps you connected, like "strands" intermingled to form a strong bond in your "*God Kingdom Relationship*."

This measure of worship once put into full gear equips you to follow God's command without displeasure and discontentment.

Rather instead, your obedience is a display on a mantle that radiates your deepest and utmost pleasure to follow wherever He leads and to do whatever He says.

Do you remember in the beginning of this chapter the revelation we gradually unfolded on some of the truths to our repentance?

If so, I want to revisit this topic once more to redirect our attention on the effects of this action taken and to reveal how God's Power and Glory is the "adhesive glue" that preserves this magnificent and rewarding *God Kingdom relationship*.

Please join me as we pull back the curtains to reveal more of God's glorious light on how to draw nearer to God in the times when you become weary, weak, discontented, condemned, frazzled and flustered by the hardships you encounter in the phases of your journey.

When things in life don't always go as you would like, we sometimes accept the wrong actions for our cure and immediately we are consumed in our feelings of regret, resentment and sometimes have a tendency to hide from our sin and seclude away from the only One that can help us- and that One of course is, Jesus. *So don't run away!*

When you find yourself in this predicament and your sins seem to weigh you down, *run to God.*

Remember child of God, He is our "safety net" and our refuge in the time of trouble.

Whenever you "miss the mark" confess to God your erroneous ways and wrongdoings and stay in sweet communion with Him, to receive forgiveness, restoration, cleansing and most importantly, to receive a peace that surpasses your knowledge beyond human understanding.

Tell me, what more could we ever ask for or need.

Best of all, God's grace and love for you forever remains the same yesterday, today and forever in spite of the Satan's false accusations made against you.

So what does repentance really mean?

"Repentance" is defined as a change of attitude towards God and His precepts.

The truest "acid" test and "evident" proof of our Godly repentance is demonstrated when the believer completely turns away from his sin by first making a quality decision to put himself in total agreement by aligning his will for his life in submission to God's Word.

When this practice soon becomes second nature to you, it is then that the *power of agreement* and harmony can operate successfully in your relationship with The Father.

The Bible carefully instills in the heart of the believer that without this kind of sentiment being cultivated in a relationship to follow God, there is no real friendship, communion or fellowship that can exists between man and God.

The purpose of the question that appears in the book of Amos 3:3 proposes a question:

"Can two walk together except they be agreed?"

This was designed to show us, the believer who walks in the ways and purposes of God's ordinances, that there is power and perfect unity in walking in agreement.

True believers who choose to walk with God in this manner, are those whose hearts are receptive to God's perspectives.

When we make decisions of quality to live our lives in compliance to God's Will (The Word of God) we are indeed by all means considered, the *"blessed ones"* to experience the vastness of His gracious presence, manifested love, favor and above all- the nearness of God in ways which words cannot describe!

Having taken all of these conditions into consideration, one will soon discover and experience how possible that it is for God to communicate *heart to heart, face to face,* and *soul to soul* with any believer!

Let's center our undivided attention on Psalm 32:5-6 and view how we are to acknowledge God and come to repentance.

King David candidly cried out unto the Lord as he repented by stating first and most importantly as we read in verse 5 with these words:

> **"I acknowledge my sin unto thee and mine iniquity have I not hid. I said, I will confess my transgressions unto the Lord; and thou forgave the iniquity of my sin. For this shall every one that is godly pray unto thee in a time when thou may be found: surely in the floods of great waters: they shall not come nigh unto him."**

This frequent line of communication with God concerning repentance leaves room for the windows of heaven to continually be open in the believer's life.

When we detach and shun away from sin it no longer rules or has dominion over us and by doing so, such wonderful rewards lie ahead as we learn to trust and constantly depend on Him!

Other various avenues that have been predesigned for us to communicate with God are mentioned below.

These avenues that have been made available consists of *supplications* and *requests* that are made known unto God, *memorial prayers*, *petitions*, *declarations* and *statements of confessions* all of which have the supernatural ability to reach the heart of God!

Let's take a look at some examples from the Word of God and evaluate how the believer relates to God in prayer by way of *supplication*.

In order that we may gain a better understanding of what it means to supplicate before God, let's first find out exactly what does this word mean.

The word "*supplication*" means to plead, to make humble entreaty, to implore or to call out loudly as though you are begging to get someone's attention, such as God's.

We are to plead and make humble entreaty to God until we sense His presence and capture His undivided attention.

In the book of Psalm 5:1-3, 7 King David gained the attention of God out of desperation as a means of connecting to Him through this humble appeal.

> "Give ear to my "words" O Lord, consider my meditation." Hearken unto the voice of my cry, my King and my God: for unto thee will I pray. My voice shalt thou hear in the morning and in the morning will I direct my prayer unto thee and will look up."

Another enlightening scriptural reference that highlights how affectionately King David supplicated unto God is also recorded in the book of Psalm 17:6 that recites:

> "I have called upon thee, for thou wilt hear me, O God: incline your ear unto me, and hear my speech."

King David spoke to God candidly about his emotions, his personal challenges, his erroneous ways, his fears, his victories and aspirations that strongly supports that it is indeed possible to have free access and also constant dialogue with God, The Father as a friend.

One would have to ask himself the question, "Am I more transparent with my friends about my life than I am with God?"

For some, many share more with their friends than they do with God and perhaps the reason behind that may be because of fear and a lack of trust which is all by choice rather than by faith!

God's desire is to be actively involved in every aspect of our lives so that we can experience His goodness day by day!

"O taste and see that The Lord is good, blessed is the man that trust in him."   Psalms 34:8 KJV

Learning the art to trust God with our entire lives pave the way to a tranquil place of rest and peace that causes one to hear God's voice and to walk ever so closely with Him. David was indeed a perfect recipient of God's presence surrounding him at all times who saw God's provision for his life continually!

Secondly, King David not only purposed in his heart to practice being transparent in his conversations with God; but it's also quite evident how desperately in need he was for God to intervene on his behalf.

He acknowledged God to be the essential fiber of his being in order to inhale and to exhale.

The apostle Paul recorded his thoughts by expressing his need for God's presence as referenced in Acts 17:27-28 that professes:

"We should seek the Lord, if haply we might feel after him, and find him, though he be not far from every one of us: for in him we live and move and have our being; as certain also of your own poets have said for we are also his offspring."

David's total dependency for God was the driving force behind his motivation to seek, inquire, and to find solace for his soul.

His diligence to call on God created such a closeness that was unlike any other relationship he had ever experienced!

There was absolutely nothing that took place in David's life whether good or bad that he tried to hide from God.

As a matter of fact, all throughout the book of Psalms we conclude that there was no obstacle that was able to prohibit the freedom he had gained in his times of communing with God.

The Bible records another profound passage that highlight David's yearning in his search of seeking a deeper experience in connecting to God's presence which is found in Psalms 28:2, 6 KJV.

> **"Hear the voice of my supplications when I cry unto thee when I lift up my hands toward thy holy oracle. (verse 2)**
> **Blessed be the Lord, because he hath heard the voice of my supplications." (verse 6)**

Let's press forward as we evaluate other examples given to us in the Word of God that uncovers this approach and look to see how we can practically apply it in our very own prayer lives.

As we look to the book of II Kings 20:1-3 it proves that we are never in control of our circumstances but that we must fully trust in God's control.

This account that has been recorded tells us that King Hezekiah had become sick unto death and that a prophet, by the name of Isaiah came to him with a word from the Lord.

King Hezekiah was told by Isaiah to begin to set his house in order and should he choose to rebel, he would surely die.

Can you imagine how he must have felt? I am quite certain that he must have had a mixture of emotions to being afraid, of felling terrified, devastated, shattered and distraught!

As we continue to read throughout this chapter we find Hezekiah in despair as he wept by turning his face to God in hopes that He would hear his humble plea in granting him healing and that his life would be redeemed from destruction.

This very next verse of scripture we are about to take a look at expresses the king's thoughts that are directed towards God as he soberly reminds HIM of his faithful deeds in hopes to avoid the punishment of death.

King Hezekiah connected to God in this way by saying:

> **"I beseech thee O Lord remember now how I have walked before thee in truth with a perfect heart and have done which is good in thy sight and Hezekiah wept sore."**   **II Kings 20:3**

The word of the Lord in response to his requests made known is found in verses 5-6 that reads:

> **"…I have heard thy prayer, I have seen thy tears: behold, I will heal thee: on the third day thou shall go up unto the house of the Lord and I will add unto thy days fifteen years……."**

These passages of scriptures shared are prime examples as to how the believer can relate to God by exercising his faith to unfold greater possibilities of God's magnificent power.
It also serves as a comfort and is the foundation to our security in knowing that God is forever devoted to His immutable Word.

God's Word declares that with long life shall we be satisfied and that God will show us His great salvation.
                                              (See Psalm 91:16.)

This developed skilled form of communication amazingly brought triumph, restoration and victory back into Hezekiah's relationship with God, so much to the point where he was granted fifteen additional years added to his life!

It is quite evident that Hezekiah's struggle prior to giving birth to the vision to be made completely healed that years may be added on to his life took faith, steadfastness and sheer confidence in God's promise made to him. Hezekiah quickly learned how to worship God in spirit and in truth at a crucial time in his life when he needed it most.

His greatest blessing arose in his life when he came to understand the abundance of God's great grace (unmerited favor) that was released on his life in spite of his previous erroneous ways. Hezekiah was the "epitome" of King David's song that is expressed through the emotions given over to salty tears and brokenness which cleared the way to God's caring heart. This fascinating approach that Hezekiah used to gain the attention of God had become the basis to his language used during prayer as he pursued God's tranquil Presence.

The notorious psalm most of us are familiar with that expresses the anointed king David's plea to God in showing him mercy is a model prayer that expresses in similar ways the conduct of Hezekiah's repentance to God as found in the book of Psalm 51.

His desperate plea that resounded loudly in the ears of God, escalated him to plateaus of peace, tranquility, long life, ease and purity of heart that connected him closer to God.

The eight pleas to David's prayer of repentance has been recorded in this fashion that recites:

1. Have mercy upon me, according to thy loving kindness: according unto the multitude of thy tender mercies blot out my transgressions.

2. Wash me thoroughly from mine iniquity and cleanse me from my sin.
3. Purge me with hyssop and I shall be clean: wash me, and I shall be whiter than snow.
4. Make me to hear joy and gladness: that the bones which thou has broken may rejoice.
5. Hide thy face from my sins and blot out all mine iniquities.
6. Create in me a clean heart O God: and renew a right spirit within me.
7. Cast me not away from thy presence; and take not away thy holy spirit from me.
8. Restore unto me the joy of my salvation; and uphold me with thy free spirit. For thou desire not sacrifice, else would I give it: thou delight not in burnt offerings.

The sacrifices of God are a broken spirit: a broken and contrite heart, O God, thou will not despise."
(See Psalm 51:1, 2, 7-12, 16-17.)

As heirs and joint heirs to The Kingdom of God we must be willing to persevere without wavering and staggering in unbelief regardless of how arduous the situation may be.

Just think what would have happened if Hezekiah had received the prophecy that was spoken through Isaiah and he reluctantly failed to cast his care upon the Lord in prayer as he pleaded for his life. Yet instead, he reached out to God and tapped into the abundant provision that was made available for him by devoting his life back to the God that so loved him.

The Word of God admonishes us carefully to:
"Cast not away therefore your confidence, which hath great recompense of reward. For ye have need of patience, that, after you have done the will of God, ye might receive the promise." Hebrews 10:35

In the book of Psalms it gives us this unassailable promise: "Those who sow in tears shall reap in joy and he who continually goes forth weeping, bearing seed for sowing, shall doubtless come again with rejoicing, bringing his sheaves with him." Psalm 126:5-6 KJV

In the New Testament of the King James Version of The Bible you will find in Hebrews 11:6 that promises the believer a guaranteed reward system designed by God for those who choose to diligently seek Him by faith that declares:
"But without faith it is impossible to please him: for he that cometh to God must believe that he is, and that He is a re-warder to those that diligently seek Him."

The second avenue provided by God for the believer to *reach* and *relate* to him is through the proven gateway of memorial prayers.

Memorial prayer can be defined as a written reminder for things worthy of remembrance accompanied with a petition as we approach God in our time of fellowship.
A perfect example of such a prayer is found in the book of I Samuel 1:11 that describes the earnest and most heartfelt emotions of a woman whose greatest desire was to give birth to a child that she could call her very own.
We recall this story of a woman by the name of Hannah who was barren, mocked, grieved and despondent that miraculously found a way to boldly petition God to open her womb. I believe Hannah was tenacious in her approach as she articulated her faith in spite of the adverse circumstances that life had presented to her.
Hannah set her sights on a higher prize, ran her race and set a projector to reach her goal to having a child!
Hannah was able to reach God by knowing that "children are a heritage of the Lord and the fruit of the womb is His reward." Psalms 127:3

Hannah animatedly directed her prayer language with God out of the abundance of her complaint and grief as she was moved by The Holy Spirit.

Her *memorial prayer* uttered in the temple that day made such an impact on Eli, the priest to the point that led him to believe that Hannah had been intoxicated with strong wine. Eli proposed a question to Hannah by saying "How long will you be drunk?" but her reply brought solace by assuring him of her virtuousness.

Hannah's careful explanation that was told to Eli for her mistaken behavior was communicated with this reply: "No, my lord, I am a woman of a sorrowful spirit: I have neither drunk wine nor strong drink, but have poured out my soul before the Lord." I Samuel 1:15

Eli was convinced by telling her to go in peace and shortly thereafter declared over her life that the God of Israel would grant her the *petition* she had asked of him.

Hannah somehow knew as she took a leap of faith that surely the presence of The Lord was with her and confidently knew that God had heard her humble cry. Hannah uttered before the mercy seat of God's throne these heartfelt words that pay tribute to her memorial prayer in this fashion below.

"O Lord of hosts, if thou wilt look on the affliction of thy handmaid and remember me and not forget thine handmaid, but will give unto thine handmaid a man child, then I will give him unto the Lord all the days of his life and there shall not a razor shall come upon his head."

I Samuel 1:11

The Word of God declares to us in Isaiah 7:9 these words: …. "If you will not believe than surely you shall not be established."

Hannah came to God believing that her prayer was heard, received and answered prior to the manifestation of being able to give birth to a child that she had so desperately pleaded for.

Somehow, Hannah got a hold of walking by faith and not by sight and was comforted in spite of her shame that *when all else failed God's Word prevailed!*

Let's take a closer look at the progression of her breakthrough from God over in the next few verses where it reads:

> "...And they (meaning Elkanah and Hannah) rose up in the morning and worshipped before the Lord... and the Lord remembered her..."

This amazing reward that was granted to her demonstrated God's open willingness and compassion as a response to her memorial prayers that reached God.

(See I Samuel 1:19.)

God was both able and willing to give Hannah the keys that would unlock the doors to her dilemma. As she extended her plea up towards heaven, Hannah was able to hear from God.
This created a specific pathway that would lead her into fruitfulness and reigning victory.
God responded to Hannah's specific need and presented her with this request- a man child, Samuel by name.
Our God who is full of compassion and tender-loving kindness purposely went about to do her good just to make her happy!
God did it for Hannah and He will do it for you!

Our *memorial prayers* unto God are recalled and recognized by Him when we render our all unto Him just as Hannah did.
"Are you putting God's Word back into His remembrance?" Hannah did and so can you!
Start today by executing and releasing the promises of God's word in discovering the authority that has been given to you as God's beloved!

The fourth avenue that God has made available for the believer to have free access to reach Him is by proclamation of written *petitions*.

Have you ever asked yourself the question, "Why is it necessary to petition God?"

But before we delve into answering that question, let us search to find a proper definition of the meaning to the word *petition*.

In accordance to Webster's Dictionary, it defines the word *petition* as an earnest request, an entreaty to beseech or to plead cause with a formal written request addressed to a person in authority.

The answer to the second question is found in the book of Isaiah 43:26 [**AMP**] where God commands us to:

"Put Me in remembrance (remind Me of your merits): let us plead and argue together.

Set forth your case, that you may be justified (proved right)."

It is a command from God to the Body of Christ that serves as a means of proclaiming His intention to hear us and to respond to our pleas as a Loving Parent.

God wants more than anything just to hear from you, His Beloved!

His *eagerness* to be able to have *communion* with us on a daily basis is His greatest desire. He longs to be both our *guide* and our *counselor* as we start each day and the *cushion to our pillow* as we whisper softly to say to Him good night!

A life that is dedicated to continuous communication with God is a life that escapes the many plotted dangers of the enemy.

This type of intimate and personal relationship brings back to mind fond memories of my beloved mother when she was on this earth.

I can remember the times when she and I would talk every day and she would encourage me in my times of hardships. My mother was a firm believer in The Lord, and she would yield to God to use her on several occasions to minister His love-spoken through His Word.

The words of encouragement that was released from her very heart were words that had the power to soothe, heal and bring great comfort to my weary spirit.

It is hard for me to imagine today, that if it was not for God's grace and mercy and my mother's proper Godly wisdom that she fostered me with, where would I be?

My mother's devotion to me was uncompromising and her relentless unconditional love shown was the needful necessity in my life that miraculously kept me afloat!

As we spoke to one another from day to day it seemed as though the time well spent was never enough.

There were many times we wished that our conversations would never end!

This is exactly how God feels as He speaks to us when we make Him to be our first love, confidant, friend and Lord.

There is another profound command that has been given to us that is found in the book of I John 5:14 **[brackets are mine]** which declares:

"And this is the confidence that we have in him, that if we ask anything according to his will **[God's Word]** he hears us: and we know that he hears us, and whatsoever we ask, we know that we have the *"petitions"* that we desired of him."

King David, one of the greatest men during his era- was exemplary of this avenue in *relating* and *reaching* God many times throughout his writings in the book of Psalm.

One in particular is found in Psalm 20:4-5 **[AMP]** that reads:
> **"May he grant you according to your hearts desire and fulfill all your plans.**
> **We will shout in triumph at your salvation and victory, and in the name of our God we will set up our banners. May the Lord fulfill our petitions."**

King David realized that his first step towards gaining victory in warfare was to trust in the mercy and grace of God.

This same attitude must kindle in our spirits as well in knowing that He will preserve our lives, and cause us to triumph in this world. King David purposefully made God his praise and His name his trust by way of diligently and consistently petitioning God in prayer.

God both beseeches and encourages every believer to put Him in remembrance of His word at all times.

Giving voice to God's Word creates an atmosphere that is charged with the evident power of His presence that allows God to speak and to be heard.

This act of boldness executed by a believer strengthens the relationship with God in greater dimensions causing Him to be a constant companion and at best, your confidant, your victory and closest friend!

Another beautiful account that was given for our exhortation to make *petitions* before God was the example set by Queen Esther.

As we read this passage in Esther chapter 5 beginning at verses 3-8 we find that here stood a woman, the queen who was full of grace and splendor, this queen graciously went before the king with humility, boldness and also with a *petition* in her hand in hopes to free her people from being slain, destroyed and sold as slaves by the wicked servant of the king, by the name of Haman.

The story tells us that it came to pass on the third day that Esther decked herself in royal apparel and stood in the inner court of the king's house in hopes to gain his attention. The king beheld her beauty and was most pleased and mesmerized as he saw her from afar standing in the yard.

Consequently, she was personally invited to enter his courts as he held out his gold stick that was in his hand. Esther extended her hand to touch the end of the golden stick and it was at this very moment where she found favor and grace in his sight to present her request to the king!

Esther's delightful presence on that particular day had made such an impact on the king, that it moved him with compassion and granted her a promise to give her anything that her heart desired.

This amazing account of Esther's life renders homage of how she obtained and maintained favor in the king's sight. Imagine this if you will, you have been given the highest and most distinguished honor by the Queen of England a personal invitation to enter into her royal courts for in depth conversation and for tea to discuss a vision plan that you, being the ambassador have implemented on behalf of your country.

As you draw near to the Queen-she in turn, discerns the aura of your presence that surrounds you and quickly summons you to partake with her in sharing the same ordained authority, privileges and equal rights over provinces where she triumphantly reigns!

Tell me, what would you do if you were put in this very same position?

I strongly believe the answer to this question would be that you too, would act graciously very much like Esther who in turn nobly accepted the invitation as a symbol of mutual agreement in sharing authority that was given to her by the king.

This is analogous to the covenant we have with Jesus.
To put it simply, a covenant is a mutual binding agreement and a promise that is shared between two or more parties that in essence, declares that because God is eternal, the oath between the two parties can never be broken.

This precious gift of salvation unto eternal life that God gave us through His Only Begotten Son, Jesus Christ and the covenant we have with Him, is by far the purest and truest promise ever known to God's beloved!

According to Hebrews 9:12 God's promise of eternal blessings is bestowed upon the righteous in accordance to one's faith in the saving blood of His Son, Jesus Christ.

> "Neither by the blood of goats and calves, but
> by his own blood he entered into the holy place,
> having obtained eternal redemption for us."

Did you see what Jesus did for you Beloved?
Believe and know that He redeemed you and made you the righteousness of God in Christ Jesus! Glory to God!

If this seems hard for you to grasp, Beloved, then please take just a moment and meditate on Paul's words that he spoke in II Corinthians 5:21. In fact, I suggest that you read this aloud right this very moment as a means to activate this blood covenant you now have with God, The Father, The Son and The Holy Spirit, as One.

Please note that the **[Brackets are Mine]for emphasis purposes only.**

> "For **[Put your name here]** unrighteousness
> Jesus became sin for **[Put your name here]**,
> who knew no sin that**[Put your name here]**
> might be *made the righteousness of God in him*."

Now can you understand from studying the book of Esther why King Ahasuerus was so generous towards Esther?

King Ahasuerus extended, exchanged and transferred his power over into the hands of Queen Esther for her powerlessness which by accepting the royal scepter as a sign of authority to rule as an equal partner with the king, had the power to eliminate and to demolish any and all other weak vices that she had in times past operated in and had become accustomed.

In the depths of this amazing covenant, something so magnificent happened. Because of the covenant that had taken place between The king and Esther, this transaction had become sealed into a law that could not be reversed which made it effortless for her petition to be established, approved, and granted for her people.

As an equal partner in this magnificent covenant, with it- came the undeniable possibilities of fierce unquenchable confidence, unstoppable faith, and in the areas of Esther's life where there was once fear, it was replaced with sheer determination, faith and a boldness that liberated and permitted Esther to surpass and conquer all!

Queen Esther no longer was just an ordinary woman but she was now seen and respected the more as *The Queen* who both ruled and reigned in her kingdom.

You see, Esther was a queen before she was chosen to be the queen to king Ahasuerus before the foundation of time.

It was as though she had been naturally prepped for the role to be a queen before she had entered Shushan the palace, to the house of the women unto the king's chamberlain for purification purposes.

This very next profound passage that we about to explore exposes the tactics of Esther's wisdom used in her approach to the king.

It justifies how as believers, we are to come before God with *petitions* by making our request known unto Him without reservation, aloofness or fear, but come before Him with boldness, courage and confidence.

The book of Proverbs 28:1 plainly asserts this serenity of mind for those who will not be daunted by the difficulties that faces them.

Begin to see yourself in this passage of scripture and stand firmly on your covenant promise and believe that you are what God's Word says you are......BOLD as a lion!

> "The wicked flee when no man pursues them,
> but the[uncompromisingly] righteous are as *bold* as lions."

Follow me closely as we continue to explore Esther's plan of action in believing God to intervene at the appointed time in telling the king what it was that she had wanted. The story tells us as they were drinking wine, the king asked Esther this certain question:

> "What will you have Queen Esther?"
> "What is your request?" It shall be given you,
> even to the half of the kingdom it shall be
> performed and Esther answered, If it seem
> good unto the king, let the king and Haman
> come this day unto the banquet that I have
> prepared for him. If, I have found favor in
> the sight of the king, and if it please the king
> to grant my petition, and to perform my request
> I will do tomorrow as the king hath said."
>
> (See Esther 5:6-8.)

During the time of the meal, the king once again promises to give Esther whatsoever her heart desired, yet she stood still and did not at this time reveal to him what she truly wanted.

Instead, Esther had another plan of action and that was to invite both the king and Haman to another meal the very next day.

I believe she was waiting on God's lead and perhaps felt that it would be best to ask the king to grant her request the following day. Esther proceeded to invite Haman to be present only to expose his evildoings before the king in hopes that he would not avoid and dodge judgment.

Let's continue to read further in chapter seven starting at verse 2 where the king asks Queen Esther on that second day what was her petition.
In spite of the dismal dilemma that faced Esther and her people, (The Jews) she was able to pierce the heart of the king in the depths of her very own emotions that were tenderly expressed with these few words as we read in verse three.

> "If I have found favor in thy sight, O king and if it pleases the king, let my life be given me at my petition and my people at my request."

Queen Esther asked for two very important requests to be fulfilled by the king. Obviously, what she had to say brought curiosity to the king and would have made Haman quite fearful of this truth being told to the king.

The king's reaction to Esther revealing the name of the wicked one that was ruthlessly annihilating and destroying her people, (The Jews) was none other than Haman who was sentenced to death and to be hung on the gallows.
The Bible records that King Ahasuerus gave Esther all of the property that had previously belonged to Haman, which permitted Esther to come boldly before the king as she found solace to announce that Mordecai was her uncle.

Once King Ahasuerus heard this news, he took off his ring and placed it on the finger of her uncle, Mordecai.

This kingly type action served notice to the Jews and those in the kingdom as a bold display of transferred authority that was immediately placed into the hands of Mordecai as the new law maker for his people. A new covenant was now birthed between the King and Mordecai that changed his life and the lives of his people for generations.

The king also gave Esther the responsibility to rule and to have total access of Haman's property as a token of his love, admiration and respect.
God was continually showing Esther His grace and His favor in times when she needed it most.

I strongly urge you to begin today by making this bold declaration when you need a reminder that God loves you and how He will move mountains out of your way in a time when you need Him most as you rely on Him alone in fulfilling your earnest petitions.

Repeat this prayer confession after me:
Father, I praise and thank you for accepting and loving me as your own dear child. You are my glory and the lifter of my head. Your Word promises me that You, Father have the kings heart in the palms of your hands as the rivers of water and that You can turn it towards me for my good whithersoever You will over my life.
Thank you Father, that much favor and much more grace guides me in all wisdom and truth. My life is a life of free favors that causes me to have victory in all affairs and situations in this present life.
I receive by faith these promises, as an extension of the covenant You have given to me as a token of Your genuine expression of the Love You have for me, Your Beloved, Your Handmaid, and most importantly as Your Child of The Most High.
In the Matchless and Mighty name of Jesus I pray.   Amen.

Let us learn from this lesson that we are to be "doers" of God's Word, to be bold, full of faith when we pray and to keep our eyes on the prize and never lose heart.

It is here at the throne where you will find God, Who is Love Mercy and Grace!

Let's turn our attention now towards discovering the power that God has given to every Man to use as a means of declaring His Word-*The Mouth*.
The life of Moses, I believe is one of the greatest and most dramatic stories in all of the Old Testament and some of the things that he endured we can all certainly learn from by his example and hopefully incorporate them into our own personal walk with the Lord.

As we read some of the few highlights of his story particularly in the book of Exodus 4:11 we find a confused Moses, who steadily questioned God as to whether or not He has called and chosen the right candidate for the job.
Moses opened his mouth and proceeded to tell God repeatedly all of the excuses as to why he believed that he was not the right man for the position.

His excuses given were many. Some of the excuses articulated by Moses as he spoke to God, was how he saw himself as; 1) not being well versed, 2) not being eloquent in speech, 3) that he was not poised and lacked self-assuredness and lastly, 4) he elaborated continuously that he was vexed with stammering lips. Then suddenly, the Maker and Creator of Moses's mouth responds back by saying these powerful words with *His Mouth* declaring to Moses:

"Who has made man's mouth? Or who makes the mute, the deaf, the seeing, or the blind? Have not I, the Lord? Now therefore, go, and I will be with your mouth and teach you what you shall say."

In spite of Moses' lack of confidence during this early stage in his walk with God, He was still able to successfully use him to deliver His instructions as to what was to be done for the children of Israel, as he recited to them on two stone tablets, The Ten Commandments.

As we learn from this small but yet impactful lesson from Moses's example, let us be mindful of the fact that if God calls you to do an assignment be assured that HE has qualified you to do the job and that HE sees the end from the beginning to all things!

In addition to Moses assignment in delivering the specific laws that God desired for the children of Israel to abide by, God manifested His Presence on Moses in such a glorious way that caused the people to murmur amongst themselves as they listened to his words that were given to him by the Great I AM.   Proverbs 18:4 [**AMP**] declares:

"The words of a man's mouth are as deep waters, and the wellsprings of wisdom is (dispersed from his mouth) as a flowing brook."

"What are you declaring in your life today as God gives you instruction?" "When was the last time you made some type of official announcement to God or stood in His Presence giving voice to His word with your mouth by way of *declarations* that moved the heart of God?"

Unlike the personality of Moses, King David was well versed in how he *related* and *reached* God with words that just seemed to fluently flow from his heart and out of his mouth without hesitation. The psalmist quickly learned how to wait patiently, to trust and believe God to be the Rock of his foundation.   King David foretells of that liberty and work of redemption in this way which is found in Psalm 40 beginning at verse ten and it reads:

"I have not hid thy righteousness within my heart:
I have *declared* thy faithfulness and thy salvation:
I have not concealed thy loving-kindness and thy truth from the great congregation."

The Psalmist also understood clearly that he had sin in his life and was plunged into a horrible pit of miry clay, out of which he was sinking deeper and deeper without having the power to pull himself out.

But amazingly what he did discover was the mercy of God. From God alone, David expected relief, deliverance and His grace to help him during the darkest times of his most un-worthiest state of being.

We understand that there is enough power in God both to help and to sustain even the weakest, and by faith we must be willing to receive His unmerited favor and grace that has been extended to us in embracing the unredeemed.

Psalm 119: 26-27 shows how open confession should be a believer's best practice in drawing God nearer to him.

There is nothing that can bring more ease and honor to a man than to be honest in acknowledging and confessing his sins before God.

David felt this way and in this verse he pleads for God's full forgiveness and hence pleads to be taught by the greatest Teacher of all, God Himself as to how he should live holy. David's bold cry to God frequently followed this pattern.

"I have *declared* my ways and opened my grief's to You, and You listened to me; teach me Your statutes. Make me to understand the way of your precepts; so shall I meditate on and talk of your wondrous works."   [*Italicized for Emphasis*] **[AMP]**

King David formally made known to God his sins and then proceeded to ask God to teach and to show him His ways. He declared unto God his faithfulness religiously and frequently pondered on the promises that God made with him.

David often spoke of the promises by releasing *confessions* of how marvelous God was to him and *declared* God's Word consistently without protest.

In review of all that we have learned in this particular chapter let us keep in our minds and in our hearts that the Lord hears our prayers.
The Word of God assures and comforts us in knowing that "God is far from the wicked: but he hears the prayers of the righteous." Proverbs 15:29

God's word also promises us contentment and much gain as we search the scriptures by believing that He hears our prayers, our petitions, confessions, and declarations as Psalm 10:17 proclaims with these words:

"O Lord, you have heard the desire and the longing
 of the humble and oppressed; You will prepare and
 strengthen and direct their hearts, You will cause your
 ear to hear." **[AMP]**

Our Father diligently gives heed to our pleas and despite our fears, God walks in the midst of our fiery furnaces and succors us that He has indeed heard our prayers.
I strongly encourage you to passionately *live in prayer* and to declare and confess all of your ways unto the Lord.

"For out of heaven He made thee to hear his voice,
that He might instruct thee: and upon the earth He
showed thee His great fire; and thou heard his
words out of the midst of the fire."
 (See Deuteronomy 4:36 KJV *Italics Emphasized.*)

As I began to search for other expressions of using confessions in prayer I came across another example found in II Chronicles 30:22 and verse 27.

This passage records how Hezekiah sent letters to Judah, Ephraim and Manasseh concerning the Passover.

The people could not participate because the priests at that time had not yet sanctified themselves properly prior to the Passover.

Therefore the people went throughout all Israel to make proclamations to keep the Passover unto the Lord God of Israel in Jerusalem.

Hezekiah was instrumental to God as he spoke to the Levites during the feast for seven days and made bold confessions to the Lord God of their fathers.

The priests and the Levites arose, blessed the people, and their prayers came up to God's holy dwelling place.

The believer's voices were heard by God as we learn in verse 27 which establishes the fact that yes, God hears our cry, whether it is through our supplications, our requests, memorial prayers, petitions, declarations or from our daily confessions announced by way of diligently acknowledging The Lord, God.

In light of this statement, in closing I leave you with this final passage in Psalm 145:19 KJV that recites:

" He will fulfill the desire of them that fear Him:
" He also will hear their cry, and will save them."

Chapter 3. A.. "Almighty God"

"After these things the word of the Lord came unto Abram in a vision, saying, Fear not, Abram: I am thy shield and thy exceeding great reward."
Genesis 15: verse 1

As we look unto the Lord Jesus who is the Author and the Finisher of our faith-filled prayers, we will discover how great men and women of the faith acknowledged Him, how He was introduced to them and how they experienced Him to be the **Great I Am** in their lives.

One of the most infamous stories told in The Bible from generation to generation is the call and assignment on Moses and the ministry that God ordained for his life as we read in Exodus beginning at chapter three.

Let's go directly to the same passage of scripture again where we find Moses having direct conversation and dialogue with God regarding this call while tending to the flock and he came to the mountain of God, called Horeb.

The Bible bears witness that while Moses was there that an angel of the Lord appeared unto him in a flame of fire out of the midst of a bush and the bush burned with fire but yet not consumed.

Moses, I am quite sure from reading this story must have been in a state of shock as he tried to figure out how was it that a tree could be in flames but not scorched into debris.

The scripture tells us that the Lord saw Moses and he called him by his name from out of the midst of the bush and acknowledged Himself by telling Moses who He was by saying; *Here am I.*   [*Italicized for Emphasis*]

As God gave Moses careful instructions to take off his scandals He then introduced Himself again and said to Moses these words:

"I am the God of thy father, the God of Abraham, the God of Isaac, and the God of Jacob."   Exodus 3:6

I can only assume how frightened Moses must have been because the text describes that Moses hid his face because he was afraid to look upon God.

However, in spite of his great fear to look upon God, God consoled him and assured Moses He had seen the affliction of His people in Egypt and that He had heard their cry and was aware of their deep sorrows.

Moses heard directly from out of the mouth of God which captivated his undivided attention as God later on in their conversation gave him the compass of his divine assignment to confront Pharaoh in bringing the children of Israel out of captivity in Egypt.

Moses quickly found himself doubting this arduous command given to him by saying to God, "who am I that I should go unto Pharaoh and that I should bring forth the children of Israel out of Egypt?"

"Have you ever been in a position when God speaks to you and the task that has been handed to you appears to be larger than life per say?"

You roll over and over in your mind recurrently how you are to accomplish such an assignment that God has entrusted you to fulfill while on the other hand, what we fail to grasp is the fact that God is our help and shield and we quickly lose sight of the Greater One that resides on the inside of us that will do the work and not we ourselves within our own strength.

As we follow Moses' life we read on in that very same chapter in verse 12 to find God's words of comfort given to Moses saying:

"Certainly I will be with thee; and this shall be a token unto thee, that I have sent thee: When thou hast brought forth the people out of Egypt, ye shall serve God upon this mountain."

The very next phrases spoken by Moses is key to him fulfilling God's plan for his life that is recorded in verse 13 and Moses said unto God these words:

> **Behold, when I come unto the children of Israel, and shall say unto them, The God of your fathers have sent me unto you; and they shall say to me, What is his name? What shall I say unto them?**

God never once allowed Moses' interruption of the world that he lived in to enslave his emotions from throwing him off course.

Rather instead, The God of Heaven responded both calmly and confidently in reassuring Moses repeatedly that He was with him.

Moses was rapidly being trained in becoming steady and un-moveable for the events soon to take place that was ordained for the freedom of God's people.

God had divinely and strategically mapped out every fine detail of Moses's journey ahead by encouraging him once more who He was! God replied with such authority to Moses' question of who He was in this next verse (14).

God said unto Moses, I AM THAT I AM: thus shalt thou say unto the children of Israel, I AM hath sent me unto you.
The Lord God continued to speak to Moses and said; "Thus shalt thou say unto the children of Israel, The Lord God of your fathers, The God of Abraham, The God of Isaac, and the God of Jacob, hath sent me unto you: this is my name for ever, and this is my memorial unto all generations." (verse 15).

The victorious outcome of God's people being set free from the dictates of Pharaoh's hands proved to Moses and the children of Israel that He was their "rock" and their solid defender.

There is absolutely no circumstance or situation that surrounds you, Child of God that can overtake you by presenting its grips to enslave and limit you!
We must always remember there is nothing too hard for our God and that He is sovereign in all of our life's experiences!

The closer we desire to walk and to communicate with God the easier it becomes to hear His melodious and calm voice when HE speaks.

The closer we live to God, and delight in His presence-the comfort of reclining in His peace has the supernatural ability to transform our fears and doubts into steeper heights of perpetual trust!

I can attest to these two statements to be most true.
There was a time in my life, I had to raise my son as a single mother and how many of us who have been given that charge can empathize and understand that kind of responsibility? Just the very thought of trying to do practically everything on my own at times almost seemed impossible to achieve.
At one point, I had become trapped and enslaved by spending so much time on making ends meet for my son and I that the weight of stress and worry tried to consume me-until one day I heard The Holy Spirit speak to me and He said; "Peace, be still."
From that day forward, I made a conscious decision to spend more time meditating on The Word of God, I became a member of a Bible teaching, Word based church and began to live closer to God so I could hear His promptings on how to raise a Godly son, and how to live a wholesome, productive and fearless life.
I am so much more the blessed today than words could ever convey.
When we fully commit unto Him then we can trust Him to carry us, by making our journeys less tiresome and our paths taken to be much smoother.

I perceived God as being like the *transformer*, who was able to take all of my past fears, insecurities, disappointments, sorrows, pains and failures and miraculously crushed the deeds of darkness and turned my tears into laughter again!
"Tell me, how are you spending your time with God?"
"Are you able to hear His distinct voice when He cordially introduces Himself to you?"
Sometimes it just easier to sit still in His presence and remain quiet so that you can focus on hearing only Him as opposed to hearing yourself talk.

Remember, it is often during those quiet times alone with God when He "transmits" vital information that has the ability and the power to forever change you so that your heart can become sensitized to the leading and the directing of The Holy Spirit.

Let's take a brief look at the progression of how God came to introduce Himself to a man in The Bible by the name of Jacob, who was Isaac's son and the grandson to Abraham.

The story paints a vivid portrait in Genesis 35:11 in The King James Version of The Bible of Jacob's practice to carefully listening to God and how this practice increased his ability to quickly obey the instructions that he was given to build an altar in the land of Bethel.

Reading this story was amazing, because what I discovered was that the same location God had told Jacob to build an altar; was the very same place Jacob had fled to when he was in hiding from the face of his brother, Esau.
During the time when Jacob fled from his brother, it was then at this very same location he began to recognize that it was God who answered him in his day of distress.

Jacob had come to understand that it was God who was with him that protected him from the snares of his worst enemies.

The Word of God encourages us, that because of His tender loving-kindness He shows us in spite of our flawed short-comings and rebellious ways, He still remains the same towards us and His goodness, blessings and love never ceases, not for one split second. Praise The Lord!

God had been so faithful to Jacob during his darkest hour that when he was given the assignment-he did not allow anything to prohibit him from being disobedient to God!
(See Romans 2:4)

It was quite obvious that God knew Jacob better than he had known himself. You see, God's plan all the while was to prosper Jacob and bless him to live the good life!
In the next following verse God introduced Himself to Jacob in this way by saying:

**"I am God Almighty: be fruitful and multiply;
a nation and a company of nations shall be of
thee, and kings shall come out of thy loins;
and the land which I gave Abraham and Isaac,
to thee I will give it, and to thy seed after thee
will I give the land."   Genesis 35:12**

Everything that God possesses and purposefully uses for our advantage is an extension of Himself that He gives to us as a free gift to bless us, to promote us and to favorably prosper us, just as He did for Jacob.

God is truly the *"All Sufficient and Breasty One"* who supplies every one of our needs to the fullest measure. He is the Almighty God, commonly referred to being **The Great Jehovah- El- Shaddai!**

Perhaps you may call Him by another name that only you and He are familiar with.

I have three adorable, precious little grand-daughters, and each of them have been given totally three different and separate nicknames to which I actually initiated. When I call out to each of them by their nicknames, the greatest satisfaction is that they hear my voice and they in return, cheerfully respond by giving me their undivided attention! Our Heavenly Father share the very same sentiments as we do when we call out to Him by His Holy name.

God is a brilliant conversationalist, Who is genuinely interested in everything about you.

So call on Him today and don't waste another minute to see what exciting new topics you and He can discuss and chat about in your next conversation!

Let's take a peek at some of the different names that God revealed to the Israelites that have been passed down from generations as we discover in Bible history.

All throughout The Bible, there are many accounts that salute and reverence God's name with the highest admiration. For example, Isaiah the prophet, boldly proclaimed the prophetic coming of Jesus and pronounced His name by declaring to us:

"For unto us a child is born unto us a son is given and the government shall be upon his shoulder; and his name shall be called Wonderful, Counselor, The Mighty God, The Everlasting Father, and Prince of Peace." **Isaiah 9:6 KJV**

In Genesis 15:1 God revealed Himself to Abraham as being his **shield** and **exceedingly great reward**!

From Bible history, we learn a great deal about Abraham's journey. By reading his story we can certainly empathize with him in his trials of difficult problems, failures, doubts, and weaknesses that he experienced in his life.

However, despite all the test that he had to endure, his neediness for God's provision, guidance, wisdom, peace, victories, love and much more, had become the vehicles used in his training to direct his footsteps towards maintaining a true dependence in coming to know God as being his *shield a*nd *exceedingly great reward.*

In addition to Abraham's relationship with God, he had become so transparent with God and because of this new release of liberty, Abraham came to know the deep secrets of God's true identity as Lord!

It is only when we refine the art of being transparent with God, that we are positioned for transition to take place that is ultimately, followed by transformation in our lives!

In Abraham's experiences, he came to possess such a closeness with God that intensified the capacity of both his awareness and realization of who God truly was.

Tell me, what has your most recent experience with God been like? In your times of talking to God, would you say the realization of Who He is, has become much clearer and a lot easier for you to wholeheartedly enjoy His fellowship? It is my sincere prayer for those reading this book that you will continue to open your heart to receive every good and earthly blessing that He wants to share and give to you as His fondest and most dearest friend!

Below you will find some of the many Glorious and Divine names for God. As you come to focus on God's great names-take notice of the Divine names that you use to address Him during your private time in prayer.

JEHOVAH-ELOHIM, the God who is the Creator of the heavens and earth, Who was in the beginning, the God of might and strength was another name Abraham had become accustomed to calling God.

[Refer to Genesis1:1-2]

JEHOVAH EL-SHADDAI, The God Almighty of Blessings, who is the Breasty One, Who nourishes and supplies.
Abraham came to know God as being The All- Bountiful and The All Sufficient One in the event of his son, Isaac's life. [Refer to Philippians 4:19]

Do you remember the story when God had given command to Abraham to take his only son to Mount Moriah and in this place, he was to sacrifice his son as an offering unto The LORD GOD? Yet instead, God supplied another sacrificial offering on that day by providing a ram in the bush. Glory to God!

How rewarding it is to know that our direct contact with God, The Father who is *El-Shaddai,* has not only loved us, but HE also *adopted* us into His family, and with deep uttered affection He calls you and I *His beloved* and most cherished friends!

According to Paul's teachings the Word says; "God chose us in Him before the foundation of the world that we should be holy and without blame before him in love having predestinated us unto the adoption of children by Jesus Christ to himself, according to the good pleasure of his will, to the praise of the glory of his grace, wherein he hath made us**[Brackets Mine] [you and I]** accepted in the beloved." Ephesians 1: 4-6 KJV

JEHOVAH-JIREH, The One Who sees and provides all of our needs, is also another name Abraham associated with who God was in his life which is a universal name commonly used in the Body of Christ.
[Refer to Genesis 22:14]

JEHOVAH-NISSI, Our Victory, Our Banner and Our standard! [Refer to Exodus 17:15]

JEHOVAH- El-ELYON, The Most High God, Who is the First Cause of everything, the Possessor of the heavens and the earth. The Everlasting God, the Faithful God, and the Mighty God!   [Refer to Genesis14:18-20]

JEHOVAH ADONAI, Who is our Lord and our Master. The Completely Self-Existing One!
[Refer to Hebrews 13:8]

JEHOVAH RAPHA, Our Healer and the One Who sent His Word and heals us and forgave all of our iniquities and healed all of our diseases!
[Refer to Exodus 15:23-26 AMP]
[Refer to Psalm 103:3]

JEHOVAH-SHALOM, The Lord God Who is our Peace!   [Refer to Philippians 4:7]

JEHOVAH-TSIDKENU, The Lord Our Righteousness!
[Refer to Jeremiah 23:6]

JEHOVAH-M'KADDESH, The Lord God, Our Sanctifier!   [Refer to Leviticus 20:7-8]

JEHOVAH- SHAMMAH, The Lord God, Who will never leave us nor forsake us. HE is always there for us!
[Refer to Hebrews 13:5]

JEHOVAH-ROHI, The Lord God Who is Our Shepherd that will never cause us to lack any good or beneficial thing! Hallowed be Thy name!
[Refer to Psalm 23:1]
[Refer to Matthew 6:9]

JEHOVAH- SABAOTH, The Lord of Host!
[Refer to I Samuel 17:45]

JEHOVAH El-OLAM, The Everlasting God!
                     [Refer to Genesis 21:33]
JEHOVAH El-ROI, Our Lord God that See us!
                     [Refer to Genesis 16:13]

From the very beginning in the book of Genesis and to the end in the book of Revelation, God's name is reverenced, exalted, praised and remembered as being the God who is forever faithful and true to those who call upon Him in truth.

As you make it a conscious decision to commit yourself to pray and uphold personal contact with God and by staying in constant communion with Him-you can confidently believe without doubt as it declares in the book of I Peter 3:12 **[AMP]** this valid certainty:

> "For the eyes of the Lord are upon the righteous-those who are upright and in right standing with God-and His ears are attentive (open) to their prayer. But the face of the Lord is against those who practice evil [to oppose them, to frustrate, and defeat them]."

This next scene we are about to expound on shares with us in the purest way to namely, learn how we are to bless God for His name, the revealed knowledge He has given to the Body of Christ through His Word (Will) and the expressed sufficient proof of Himself.

In the book of Nehemiah, he records the time when Ezra, the scribe gathered the people "as one man" in the streets to bring the book of the Law of Moses to minister to Israel as a direct command from God.

    As we continue to read this account we will discover how God's presence upon Ezra impacted the children of Israel in such a way that it caused eyes that were once shut to be opened to truth and hearts of men to be transformed into understanding the light of God's Word.

Ezra's first command given by God was to open the book in the sight of all the people.
When he opened the book something so remarkable took place in the lives of the people that gave them a fresh and innovative meaning to the word *joy*.

Let's go to the scriptures and see exactly what it was that changed the people's thinking and their perspective of God's spoken word.
The story tells us that when Ezra opened his mouth to read the Law of Moses that all the people stood up and he *blessed the Lord, the great God, so they read in the book of the law of God distinctly, and gave sense to the meaning of the law and caused them to understand the reading.* Ezra said unto the people, *This day is holy unto the Lord your God;* mourn not, nor weep ... *for all the people wept,* **when** *they heard the words of the law…..* then he said to them; "go your way eat the fat and drink the sweet and send portions unto them for whom nothing is prepared": *for this day is holy unto our Lord; neither be ye sorry; for the joy of the Lord is your strength and all the people went their way* and made great mirth *because they had understood the words that were declared unto them.*
(See Nehemiah 8:1-12.) *[Italicized for Emphasis]*

This story would imply to us that the people that had gathered themselves together in assembly, may not have been accustomed to hearing God's Word in the convincing manner as to how it was delivered. But, what this story does imply as a valid truth for us all, is the mere fact-that it is *Prayer that Changes Things*!
The scriptures tells us at the very moment when Ezra's voice was heard to read the sacred scroll and he began to **pray** to God, the entire assembly bowed down on their knees and fell on their faces to worship God in the beauty of holiness- and with one voice, they all responded with *great joy*!

Ezra's passionate delivery is still believed today, to be the origin that gives meaning as to why it is so important to bless God for understanding the Godly influences of HIS name, and how we can learn to adopt to have this same attitude the people displayed to both hearing and receiving God and His precepts.

In addition, we must also be willing to adapt in being led by The Holy Spirit as we listen attentively to His voice and eagerly submit to His Will through the Person of Jesus.
I strongly believe that this picturesque scene was in essence and still remains today, to be one of the most powerful and illustrative examples to describe one of the many personality traits and administration of The Holy Spirit, Who gives us complete joy, contentment and peace; because of what we know about HIM, Who HE is and who we are to HIM!

Let's take a microscopic look to see exactly what it means for a devout Christian to harness the spirit of *joy* and how it becomes the supernatural outcome of their faith, in spite of life's consequences that faces them.

In our recent research to the scripture found in the book of Nehemiah 8:10 we can conclude from its contents that; *joy* can be defined as the calm, inner strength of our spirit that gives us rest in knowing what God's blood has ratified for us, and having with it-the supernatural ability to "strip away fear and depression from the very root, depriving it of its power and influence to contain you!"

> *A believer's joy stems from the revelation in intimately knowing and understanding who God is and what He can and will do on his behalf without fail!*

An often asked question is: "How is it that joy and happiness are not equated to being the same emotions?"

The answer to this question is comparatively simple.
This second fruit of the spirit-*Joy* that is mentioned in Galatians 5:22 can easily stabilize and soothe a believer in any worst case scenario in life's most challenging moments!
It has the power within to paralyze and prevent worry and sadness to overtake a believer's stand against the enemy Satan, when he tries to plot and scheme wicked devices against you!

Joy, being unlike any other fruit of The Spirit has been meticulously and miraculously designed by God to keep us at ease to remain confident in what we believe in our hearts without staggering on the promises of God's decreed Word.
For example, a woman goes for her annual mammogram and during the screening process the lab technician notices a dark and cloudy lump on the woman's right breast.
Soon thereafter, the lab technician discreetly leaves the presence of the patient to share the x-rays with the radiologist for a more accurate diagnosis.
As a result from the x-ray examinations that were screened and meticulously studied by the radiologist, it has been discovered that this woman has stage *(2)* of breast cancer. The radiologist enters into the room of the patient to bear the bleak news of this new found disease.

The patient bravely embraces herself to receive the diagnosis from the radiologist's report and with these words she joyfully and cheerfully responded by saying confidently:
I do not fret or have anxiety about anything-(breast- screening results) nor do I have to carry this burden. I have learned how to cast all of my cares on The Lord Jesus for I know that He cares for me.
I shall not die but live to declare the works of the Lord. I release my faith with the Word of God and boldly say that He has redeemed me from this curse by bearing my sicknesses and carrying my disease in His body and by His stripes I am healed!

This woman of great faith stood firm, fixed and secure on the uncompromising Word of God in a time when she could have cried, given up hope, became bitter or even depressed with having to handle the barrel of bad news that was given to her. This certain woman's stance that she chose to employ by faith mixed with the *fruit of joy* was not once shaken because of what she understood by "watering her faith" daily with God's promises that have been addressed personally to her!
(See Philippians 4:6, I Peter 5:6-7, Matthew 8:17,
Isaiah 53:5, Psalm 118:17, I Peter 2:24.)

Contrary to the meaning of *Joy*, let us take a close look at another emotional state of being which can mean several different things to many individuals.
This emotional state of being that we will be focusing on is the virtue of *happiness*.

Happiness can easily be defined and identified by those blissful, gleeful and delightful scenarios that we oftentimes initiate at will as an act of our very own intentional efforts. A perfect illustration of this would be sitting out on the deck on a cruise ship in the mid-afternoon for leisure on a twelve day vacation to Jamaica.

As you cuddle under one of your favorite novels in hopes to read and relax in the sun, your personal waiter arrives with your order on a sterling silver platter-a virgin margarita decorated with kiwi, lime, strawberries, blueberries and a cherry on top with whipped cream and to top it off-it is handed to you in the most exquisite crystal leaded fluted champagne glass that you have ever laid eyes on!
This emotional state of sheer *happiness* that you feel at that very moment seems as though you are in heaven until all of a sudden, the fire alarm on the cruise ship has suddenly been disarmed.

Quickly, you realize that your emotions have arrested you- summoning you to become disturbed, upset, afraid, panicky, unnerved and unraveled but most importantly, this state of mind has triggered your happiness to quickly fade away due to the threat that the fire alarm brings.

Shaking frantically with fear you come to realize that your peace has been robbed and stripped away in just minutes all because of this potential danger that now faces you!

Based on this particular scenario all was going so well with the cruise until the circumstances changed for the worst and when *happiness* departed from this individual's spirit, it reminded me of the parable of the sower that Jesus ministered throughout every city and village during His ministry on earth.

I pray that you will allow The Holy Spirit to reveal through this parable the differences between having *joy* that Jesus supplies verses the emotion of *happiness*.

> *It's good to be happy*
> *but it's even better to be "joyful"*
> *in spite of any predicament that arises*
> *and being able to take comfort in knowing*
> *and understanding that God will never*
> *leave or forsake you.* (See Hebrews 13:5.)

Jesus gave this analogy about the sower sowing the seed in the book of Luke 8:5-8, 12-15 **[AMP]**.

"A sower went out to sow seed; and as he sowed, some fell along the traveled path and was trodden underfoot, and the birds of the air ate it up and some fell on the rock, and as soon as it sprouted, it withered away because it had no moisture and other seed fell in the midst of the thorns, and the thorns grew up with it and chocked it and some seed fell into good soil, and grew up and yielded a crop a hundred times as great."

Jesus' answer to the disciples questions regarding this particular parable was simply that the seed represents the Word of God.
Thus by doing so, He was able to bring more clarity to their fuddled understanding by way of simplifying every single stanza that was communicated in His teaching.

Let's take a closer look at this parable again and discover the conclusion of Jesus' teaching on the *Sower that Sowed the Word.*

"Those along the traveled road are the people who have heard; then the devil comes and carries away the message out of their hearts, that they may not believe Me as their Savior and devote themselves to Me and be saved here and hereafter.... and those upon the rock are the people who when they hear the Word receive and welcome it with joy; but these have no root... they believe for a while, and in time of trial and temptation fall away.... and as for what fell among the thorns, these are the people who hear, but as they go on their way they are choked and suffocated with the anxieties and cares and riches and pleasures of life, and their fruit does not ripen [Brackets are Mine] [*come to maturity and perfection*]... as for the seed in the good soil, these are the people who, hearing the Word, hold it fast in a just (noble, virtuous) and worthy heart, and steadily bring forth fruit with patience."

What a revelatory, life changing moment this must have been for the disciples' to have gained such vast knowledge at the time during the climax of Jesus' ministry.

The Word admonishes us in the book of James 1:5:
> **"If any of you lack wisdom, let him ask of God, who gives to all men liberally and without reproach, and it will be given to him."**

Their uncertainties deepened their total reliance on Jesus and increased their faith to higher heights!

The disciples' saw Jesus in a brighter way and passed this knowledge down from generation to generation that Jesus is by far The Greatest Teacher!

We can conclude from this teaching that the *joyful* believers' are those identified as the sower that planted good seed into the good soil, who heard the Word and holds it fast in a just, noble and worthy heart-steadily bringing forth fruit with much patience.

The *happy* believers' are those who are identified as the sower that planted upon the rock who when they hear the Word receive and welcome it with joy; but they have no root. Eventually they believe for a while and in the time of trial and temptation they fall away (withdraw and stand aloof).

Personally, I have made it my greatest aim to be counted among those that fit in the category of holding fast to the profession of faith with a just and noble heart-bearing precious fruit with joy and with patience!

What category would you say that identifies you-the Joyful believer or is it the Happy believer?

I passionately encourage you to get on the Joyful side, the side that always wins in spite of any situation that may arise.

For He is a God that passionately longs to spread His joy into your heart repeatedly in ways more than you could ever dream of!

Let's stay on the journey and learn how other men and women have singularly developed their very own personal testimonies as to how they hailed the Names of God.

For it is through their personal struggles, triumphant victories, challenges and joy of life experiences that I will elaborate on as we continue to study these stories mentioned in the Bible.

I have carefully included various Scripture references to provide additional depth for you, the reader, in hopes that it may enlighten, admonish and to encourage you.

Certain Bible messages that are used specifically over the next few pages of this chapter are quite familiar and are purposely meant to be read and carefully studied out.

May the peace of God rule over you and cause your eyes to be enlightened and your mind to be renewed to the promises of His Word.

As we come to a close there is one very profound passage of scripture that pretty much says it all as The Holy Spirit made known to Simon Peter the Supreme identity of Jesus Christ.

Together, let's gaze through each verse of scripture in this Matthew's message in the 16th chapter as we discover the most miraculous revelation that transpired with one simple question that *Jesus* asked His disciples.

Let's take a closer look to see what actually took place when Jesus and His disciples entered into the towns of a place called Caesarea-Philippi.

It was clear that Jesus wanted the disciples to learn the most important lesson in knowing and accepting who He was. Jesus asked the disciples this question:

> **"Whom do men say that I the Son of man am?"**
> And they say that thou art John the Baptist: some, Elijah; and others, Jeremiah, or one of the prophets. He said unto them, **"But whom say ye that I am?"** And Simon Peter answered and said, *Thou art the Christ, the son of the living God [Italicized for Emphasis]* and Jesus answered and said unto him, **Blessed art thou, Simon Bar-jona: for flesh and blood hath not revealed it unto thee, but my Father which is in heaven…"**   **Matthew 16:13**

Can you imagine what a time of jubilant celebration and great joy it must have been for all of Heaven to have witnessed this prophetic utterance that "burst forth" into the open with this kind of revelation that was spoken out of the mouth of this particular disciple?

This divine connection that Simon-Bar-jona had with The Holy Spirit, whose name was later changed, to be called Peter, was transforming, radical and above all-astonishing for both he and the disciples! There is another particular individual that is observed by the name of Hosea, who in his own peculiar way came to recognize God as being the **"LION OF JUDAH"** to the house of Judah, as their defense against the tribe of Ephraim.   (See Hosea 5:14.)

During Jesus time here on the earth, scripture accurately records Jesus' reputation as being the **Good Shepherd**.

He broadcasted to every city and town where **He** and **His** disciples traveled to proclaim **His** existence on a regular basis.

Increasingly, there were many religious authorities and other personalities including the scribes and the Pharisees, who resented His influence and despised **Him** for who **He** was and for the words that **He** spoke.

Come with me as God draws us by His Spirit in making known to us who He is from this open passage of communication. Then said Jesus unto them again;

> **Verily, verily, I say unto you,**
> *I am the door of the sheep.*   verse 7.
> *I am the door* **by me if any man**
> **enters in, he shall be saved, and**
> **shall go in and out, and find pasture.**
>   verse 9.
> *I am the good shepherd:* **the good shepherd**
> **gives His life for the sheep.**   verse 11.
> *I am the good shepherd,* **and know my sheep,**
> **and am known of mine."**   verse 14.
>   *[Italicized for Emphasis]*

Notice from this parable the solicited insight Jesus freely gave to the multitude as He articulated the very nature and essence of who God is!

Although many that were present denied who Jesus was and chose to spread malicious gossip that He was vexed with demons and that He certainly could not have been the Christ were far from the truth.

These false allegations failed miserably and never once were successful in subjugating Jesus in His proclamation to the world as being the *Good Shepherd!*

To King David, God was, still is and forever always will be **THE RESTORER OF LIFE**, meaning that God is able to bring back any condition of any sort or kind to its former state-He makes restitution on behalf of every believer.

Eloquently spoken by King David we read in the book of Psalm 23:3 where he declared that God was able to restore his soul (mind, will, and his emotions) when he sought His counsel in making wise decisions.

In the book of Psalm 89:26 it assures the believer of this one thing about King David's confidence in God's presence being real in his life and it reads:

> **"Thou art my father my God and the rock of my Salvation."**

In the book of Song of Solomon 2:1 Jesus is analogous and metaphorically compared in the similitude of

> **"ROSES OF SHARON AND THE LILIES OF THE VALLEY."**

In chapter one in the last recorded book of The Bible Jesus speaks of Himself in verse 8 in Revelation as being:

> **"ALPHA AND OMEGA,"**
> **"The beginning and The Ending, which is, and which was, and which is to come The ALMIGHTY."**

According to the Amplified version of The Bible in the book of Revelation 22:16 Jesus spoke of Himself as being
> **"THE ROOT- [Bracket Mine][Meaning the Source] AND THE OFFERING OF DAVID, THE RADIANT AND BRILLIANT MORNING STAR."**

John the Baptist, who was the cousin to Jesus recurrently announced to his followers to boldly proclaim that Jesus was **The Lamb of God** who, would come to take away the sins of the world as it is written in St. John's gospel beginning at chapter one and verse twenty nine.

In John 4:14 Jesus illustratively used this simple analogy to describe Himself as being identical to *"pure water"* (the essential nourishment that is needed to sustain our lives).

In the next content of scriptures written for our learning Jesus said:

> **"But whosoever drinks of the water that I shall give him shall never thirst; but the water that I shall give him shall be in a well of water springing up into everlasting life."**

When we allow God to fill us with His living Spirit, then are we able to spiritually capture the divine revelation to Jesus' words when He spoke to His disciples and said; "he that believes on Me, as the scripture has said, out of his belly shall flow rivers of living water.

(See John 7:38.)

Having Jesus as a friend is one of life's most satisfying rewards, and without Him our lives would be most miserable and mundane.

Paul eloquently articulates in I Corinthians 15:19 exactly what his life would be like not to have Jesus as the center of his joy that is expressed in these few powerful words:

> "If in this life only we have hope in Christ,
> we are of all men most miserable."

The believer's hope is not invested in any other entity, man, gold, silver, diamonds, fame or money, nor is it in any other creature, but in Christ alone as our surety! Amen and so be it.

Another emphasis placed on Jesus identity is sought out in John 15:1 when Jesus said;

> **"I am the true vine, and my Father is the husbandmen."**

In another particular account recorded in John 8:12 Jesus had just defended the woman that was caught in adultery and His remark addressed to the angry crowd was with these powerful words.

> **" I am the Light of the World he who follows Me will not be walking in the dark, but will have the Light which is Life."** [AMP]

Jesus' testimony of pronouncing who He was created such a deep awareness to those that opposed Him, but yet all the while, He still remained a great mystery to many that witnessed His presence!

Another infamous and beautiful illustration that depicts the character of who Jesus is has been written in John's gospel beginning at chapter fourteen and verse six.

Jesus clearly uttered these very words by saying to the disciple Thomas:

> **"I am the way, the truth, and the life: no man cometh unto the Father, but by Me."**

According to John's account Jesus who was human, understood both eternal life and death.

In this next chapter of John 11:25-26 Jesus spoke to Martha regarding Lazarus, her brother's death by comforting her with these words saying: **"I am the resurrection, and the life: he that believeth in me, though he were dead, yet shall he live and whosoever liveth and believeth in me shall never die. Believeth thou this?"**

As we turn our attention over to John 6:47-48 Jesus said unto the Jews that were standing near who was murmuring falsely against Him by stating who He was by saying:

> **I assure you most solemnly I tell you, he who believes in me (who adheres to, trusts in, relies on, and has faith in Me) has now possessed eternal life. I am the Bread of Life [that gives life- The Living Bread].** **[AMP]**

True enough, Jesus' words not only pierced the hearts of those that heard Him speak, but it also brought with it countless hostile allegations from those who disapproved of His Great mission. Regardless of the matter that was at hand, Jesus unequivocally understood completely who He was and remained allegiant to His assignment without compromise!

As we revisit the book of Psalms, which is considered to be the world's most notorious collection of poems of expressing the sovereignty and greatness of God, King David exalts God's name in this way.

> **"Who is this king of glory? The Lord strong and mighty the Lord mighty in battle. Who is the king of glory? The Lord of hosts He is the king of glory."**
> **Psalm 24:8**

We can now conclude from the evidence that we have compiled through these various scriptures, that our God is a *Living Deity*, Who has proven Himself to be worthy from generation to generation.

HE is *Our Strong Tower*, *Our Buckler* and *Our Shield*, *Our Provider* and *Our Keeper* and the list goes on and on-but most importantly, ***HE IS OUR LORD!***

Our God's name is to be exalted, extoled, glorified, revered, venerated, adored, recognized, valued, honored, admired, respected, well-regarded, worshipped, esteemed celebrated, applauded, hailed and given praise in the highest and purest form!

Always remember from this lesson these assuring words as a source of encouragement:

"God's tender responsiveness to us is the very "magnetic force" that draws and compels Him nearer and it is the "strongest link" that keeps you and I connected and sealed to Him."

As you commit yourself to pray and uphold personal contact with God by staying in constant communication with Him, The Word of God declares boldly to us in the book of I Peter 3:12 this guaranteed oath:

"For the eyes of the Lord are upon the righteous (those who are upright and in right standing with God), and His ears are attentive to their prayer. But the face of the Lord is against those who practice evil [to oppose them, to frustrate, and to defeat them."
[AMP]

Chapter 4. Y.. "A Yielded Vessel"

> *"Humble yourselves therefore under the mighty hand of God, that he may exalt you in due time. Casting all of your care upon him, for he cares for you."*
> I Peter 5: 6-7

In this chapter we will both observe and critique our very own lives as it pertains to one of the most Godliest virtues known to Man- the spirit of *"humility."*

This Godly virtue of *humility*, notably as a fruit of the Spirit can be defined as a submissive act to worship that employs one's willingness and promptness in response to God's lead.

It also can be defined as the act of *"yielding"* oneself to carry out God's words by doing what God says to do without delay. For some, this concept may seem unattainable to fulfill but keep in mind, Child of God, all things are possible!

"Has there ever been a time in your life when you made a decision that was based solely on your unwillingness and refusal to yield to doing things God's way; and later when the light switch was turned on-you soon discovered that the end result to your decision was made completely out of selfish ambition, spite, rebellion and ill will towards God?"

I have just presented to you an epic scenario that is the extreme opposite of *humility*.

If you find yourself wrestling with these types of predicaments at times, I am here to encourage you that God has a better way in showing you how to avoid these pitfalls and ways to prevent you from making the wrong decisions in life.

One thing is for sure, "God can humble you" even when you think that He can't-so if this is you, just quickly repent. God loves you dearly, He is on your side, so humble yourself and do things God's way-you will be glad that you did!

This submissive act of humility in yielding to God is nothing more than surrendering your plans, your views, your ways, and your ideas over into the loving hands of God.
It is simply your acknowledgement of humbly saying to Him daily, "Father, I commit and dedicate my ways unto you, and I am willing to do whatever you tell me to do, I trust you completely, now lead me and I will follow."

Allowing God this opportunity as an act out of your obedience, now makes room by opening the doors for His divine purposes and plans to be accomplished in your life.
In Psalm 37:5 the wisdom of God's Word clearly counsels us to:
> "Commit your way to the Lord
> (roll and repose each care of your
> load on Him) trust (lean on, rely
> on, and be confident) also in Him
> and He will bring it to pass." **[AMP]**

When a believer humbly submits his will to be in total alignment with God's Will as an honor to God, his meaning-(the believer) soul (mind, will, and emotions) prospers and his life permeates with it a sense of actions, thoughts and mannerisms that genuinely express his adoration and admiration towards God.

This indeed is another *fragile fragment* of humility that we, as Christians may sometimes omit in our love walk with God in prayer, and it is the spirit of "worshipping" God.

Worship can also be defined as a genuine selfless practice that passionately embraces the awareness of God's value, by rendering reverent honor and praise for who He is and for the remarkable exploits He has done.

Submitting to God is a form of worship, that every believer should desire to live by and thus, endeavor practicing on a consistent and daily basis-for this is what pleases God!

By doing so, God welcomes your innermost responses of praise, and submission and perceives the purity of your *worship* as being analogous to a sweet smelling aroma that delightfully fumes heaven's courts!

These two spiritual tokens when executed will bridge the way for the believer to walk in "perfect liberty" that ushers God's glory in to permanently shine upon you!

Are you willing to submit to the Lord's way of doing things and receive the honor that comes from God only?

Abraham was indicative of this example as he humbly submitted to the plans and purposes of God for his life. This Godly virtue brought him honor which is in the eyes of The Lord, a great price!

His humble beginnings of the journey that brought him honor is recorded in Genesis chapter 22 beginning at verses 1-5. **[AMP]**

This poignant, emotional and heartrending story of Abraham's life captures for us a view that describes the superlative depiction of his *humility*, worship, faith, trust, obedience, loyalty, love and above all, the unending results of an eternal friendship shared with The God of the Heaven's and the Earth.

Let's get started with the instructions that had been given under God's command concerning the test of Abraham's faith.

Abraham's first instruction given by God was to take his only son, Isaac to Mount Moriah to be sacrificed for a burnt offering.

In humble obedience and submission to God's directives, **Abraham rose early in the morning to saddle his donkey, and took two young men with him and his son, Isaac.**

Abraham split the wood for the burnt offering and then began the trip to the place of which God had told him.

On the third day Abraham looked up and saw the place in the distance and Abraham said to his servants, "Settle down and stay here with the donkey and I and the young man will go yonder and worship and come again to you."

The untainted act of submission demonstrated by Abraham is considered by far, as being one of the most admirable and praiseworthy models to pattern our lives after as it relates to developing our own personal and intimate relationship with The Lord, JESUS.

As Abraham's relationship grew with God, it is vitally necessary to emphasize the fact that not only did he progressively come to learn how to trust God by faith, but how he solemnly and strongly believed every word that God had ever spoken to him, which impelled Abraham to wholeheartedly serve, submit, and worship God tirelessly.

He was fully persuaded that what God had promised to him that God would certainly do. (See Romans 4:21.)

Would it be fair to ask the question, "What would you do if God spoke and told you to start a ministry out of the basement of your home, but you didn't have a certified degree from a reputable seminary school to verify your credentials to be a minister?"

Tell me, would you follow God's instructions or not?

Because of God's grace and His faithfulness shown towards Abraham, Abraham was able to successfully pass his test that required *steadiness* to his faith, humble submission, and un-delayed obedience to God during his moments of great uncertainties and hidden doubts.

He was able to successfully give true meaning to God's commission for the believer, "to walk by faith and not by what he could see, touch, think or feel."

(See II Corinthians 5:7.)

This is what Jesus affirms *true worship* to be as cited in the Gospel of John 4:23:

"God is a spirit: and they that worship him must worship him in spirit and in truth."

I believe that after Abraham's first encounter with communing with God for the very first time, that the Spirit of God had the supernatural power to illuminate and totally disperse darkness and obscurity from out of his life instantaneously.

At that very moment, as Abraham looked unto God to be His comforter, he found such boundless freedom and a limitless liberty that set him free from the damnation and wrath of Satan's captivity.

Peace had entered in and given Abraham a new life, a new faith, a new perspective with new hope, and a new Living God that he could trust, submit to, and radically believe in!

In our times of fellowship with God, we too, can expect to experience this same peace and freedom in knowing that there is liberty in worshipping the true and Living God!

"Can you remember the last time you were in fellowship with God?"

Can you recall how peaceful and tranquil the ambience felt by being in His Presence?
I can recall how my experiences have been in just these few words that I would like to share with you.

It was one particular morning when I awaked and opened my eyes, I looked around my room and I could discern the warm presence of The Lord being there with me.

I distinctly remember saying to Him, "Good morning Jesus, how are you doing today?"
As I prepared to enter into His courts, I lifted up both of my hands reaching upward as a sign of me surrendering to His will for me to pray.
Upon my entrance into His courts, I whispered His sweet name, calling out to HIM saying, Jesus, I worship and adore you. I magnify your holy name for there is none other like YOU.
You are exalted in the earth and I praise you for being the Great and Merciful God.
YOU move mountains and YOU calm the turbulent seas, when YOU speak, the authority of YOUR voice humbles me to hear and to listen what the Spirit of the Lord will say.
I humble myself to bow down at YOUR feet and worship YOU FATHER and I bring glory to YOUR holy name.

As the time passed by, it had become quite evident that surely the sweet Presence of The Lord had drawn near.

Then suddenly, all at once, I became silent to His gentle, clement command, and softly He said to me these awe inspiring words that moved me with tears that flowed from my eyes; "Humble yourself...my child...please Humble yourself before ME.

Amen.

Humble Me

In humble submission you must yield and obey,
You must listen intently,
to hear only the words
that The Spirit of The Lord may say.

He speaks to your spirit in a clear and soothing voice
that says; I looked and I waited patiently, for
the time you would knock on My Door.
With open arms I welcome you to sit with Me,
to talk to Me, and laugh with Me
beside the tranquil peaceful shores.

As I searched your heart and I heard you speak
Quickly, I discerned from the very start
that you had become weary, tired and weak.

Oh, I saw your struggles and I felt your pain
Of the burdens you carried
I have already obtained

No More Enslavement to the Robbing of Your
Peace

*For it is **I, THE GREAT I AM**,*
Who stops and rebukes the enemy
And commands him with all authority to cease!

Give Me your life and Give Me your cares
Let Me be your Counselor to handle
all of your affairs!

Humble Me, Humble Me, Lord.

God never once intended for you and I to haul and carry needless burdens on our shoulders that Satan uses as darts to try and weigh us down, but what He did intend for us to do was that we *hurl,* our cares upon His shoulders.

"Have you ever seen a child carry a ton of bricks on his shoulders or pile them up as high as he could and place them into his toy wagon, with the attempt to tug them back and forth across the hallway near his/her playroom?" Upon observation in viewing this repeated activity of the child, quickly you discover how *fatigued* and *exhausted* they have become due to the heavy weight of the bricks that the child has *tugged* around for an expanded amount of time. Child of God, don't let this be you, cast all the weight of your worries, frustrations and cares on The Lord.
God is much stronger and more capable than you and I, so humble yourself and give it all to Jesus, you will glad that you did!

The next time you are in communion with the Lord, I humbly invite and suggest that you keep a note pad and an ink pen close by to notate any new revelations, God inspiring ideas, concepts, insights, impressions, reactions, answers to prayers or thoughts that you may have as you sit quietly in His presence.
This practical exercise will sensitize your inward witness to your born-again spirit in hearing the voice of God with clarity in understanding His leading for your life.

Please keep in mind that this is a process of continual growth that takes time to develop as you become more proficient in learning how to submit in His presence.

Let's dig a little deeper and look at another liberating life-changing passage that magnifies the total character of Jesus' stance to *submission* as inscribed in the book of John commencing at chapter seventeen.

This broad foundational truth of Jesus' unfathomable commitment encompasses the full measure of His devout and absolute adulation for God and His unconditional love for the believer.

Please come and take this journey with me as we delve into the Word of God delivered to us in John's gospel chapter 17 beginning with verses 1-10, 21-24:

Jesus spoke these words as He prayed to The Father and said: **"Father, the hour has come. Glorify thy Son, that thy son also may glorify thee, as thou hast given Him power over all flesh, that He should give eternal life to as many as thou hast given Him.**
Jesus said this is life eternal, that they may know thee, the only true God, and Jesus Christ whom thou hast sent.
I have glorified You on the earth…I have finished the work which You have given Me to do and now,
O Father, glorify thou me with thine own self with the glory which I had with thee before the world was.
I have manifested thy name unto the men which thou gavest me out of the world; thine they were, and thou gavest them me; and they have kept thy word.
Now they have known that all things whatsoever thou hast given me are of thee. For I have given unto them the words which thou gavest me; and they have received them, and have known surely that I came out from thee, and they have believed that thou didst send me.
I pray for them; I pray not for the world, but for them which thou hast given me; for they are thine; and all mine are thine, and thine are mine; and I am glorified in them."   **John 17:1-10**

"That they all may be one; as thou, Father, art in me, and I in thee, that they also may be one in us; that the world may believe that thou hast sent me; and the glory which thou gavest me I have given them; that they may be one, even as we are one; I in them, and thou in me that they may be made perfect in one; and that the world may know that thou hast sent me, and hast loved them, as thou hast loved me. Father, I will that they also, whom thou hast given me, be with me where I am; that they may behold my glory, which thou lovedst me before the foundation of the world."

John 17:21-24

Think about it Beloved, having just read this context of scripture opens our eyes even more in seeing Jesus as the perfect epic example of total submission in its purest form. Without reservation or delay throughout Jesus's ministry on earth, He humbly knelt down in a *prostrate position* to commune and to receive direction from His Father hours prior to the leading of the crucifixion.

This attitude of heart that Jesus embraced, brought sheer glory to the *finished work* that He and God had agreed upon in covenant before Jesus had entered upon the earth.

Our God is a covenant minded God who never breaches or falls short of His promises.

We are carefully reminded that the Lord our God, He is God, the faithful God who keeps covenant and mercy for a thousand generations with those who love Him and keep His commandments according to Deuteronomy 7:9 KJV.

Let's go a little further into this very same passage as we study intensely Jesus's prayer for His Disciples.

With absolute certainty as we revisit this context we can be fully convinced that the absolute love Jesus has for us is unswerving and entirely undeniable.

The words that Jesus spoke to The Father were these:
"I have manifested Your name to the men whom You have given Me out of the world. They were Yours, You gave them to Me, and they have kept Your word…now they have known that all things which You have given Me are from You… for I have given to them the words which You have given Me; and they have received them, and have known surely that I came forth from You; and they have believed that You sent Me. I pray for them I do not pray for the world but for those whom You have given Me for they are yours and all Mine are Yours, and Yours are mine, and I am glorified in them."

John 17:6-10

I want to pause for a moment and take a closer look at this one particular phrase that raised my limited knowledge to a deeper understanding to the limitless measure of love that God has for us by sharing this one unchanging truth. These comforting words that Jesus mentioned as He spoke to God were these:

"Mine are yours and Yours are mine, and I am glorified in them." verses 9-10

As a student of faith, the revelation that was given became very clear to me that we, as believers are all a part of this holy equation that JESUS was talking about in His dialogue with The Father, and The Holy Spirit.

Jesus said to me, " Beverly, everything that My Father has is Mine-and everything that I have is His-and everything that We have together as One- is absolutely Yours free-by faith!"

The moment I heard and received this revelation, no longer was I constrained to feeling as though I had to perform in order to gain benefit to Gods' blessings.

Tell me who else would have done such a marvelous thing as this outside a covenant of marriage?

We all know without reservation or doubt that when a man vows to take a woman to become his wife, that legally by the law it grants her rights and certain privileges as being the primary benefactor to every physical, and or material good that officially belongs to her spouse.

Granted by law, this very same ordinance works in the same manner accordingly for the husband.

The covenant that you and I share with God is analogous to this very same scenario in many aspects.

For instance, we derive benefit from Jesus as being our healer in exchange for our sickness, His cleansing blood to purify us from our sins[past, present and future] and by His power He took our sins and nailed them to the cross and *made* us *to be* the *righteousness of God* in Christ Jesus.

He is the Great I AM and whatever it may be that we have need of; He has already made it available in advance upon our request! (See Philippians 4:19.) You see, this holy act is the result of a spiritual law that has been established and activated as a part of your covenant when you made Jesus Lord over your life!

Let this mindset be a constant reminder to you that affirms the vast love that God has for each of us as we recite this scripture… **"God so loved the world that He gave His only begotten son and whosoever believeth in Him shall not perish but have everlasting life."**

John 3:16

As we observe the thoughts of Paul's experiences as an Apostle, we find how he uses a collection of adjectives that brilliantly unfolds Jesus' impeccable character as noted in the book of Philippians 2:5-8. Paul firmly admonishes us to "Let this mind be in you which was also in Christ Jesus, who being in the form of God thought it not robbery to be equal with God, but made himself of no reputation, and took upon himself the form of a servant, and was made in the likeness of men; and being found in fashion as a man, he "humbled" himself unto death, even the death of the cross."

What would you be willing to do when asked by God to take on an assignment that seemed to be unattainable? Would you make up excuses for not taking on the task ahead or will you just simply *submit, obey*, and become as that humble child that Jesus spoke about to the disciples located in Matthew's gospel.

My prayer is in hopes that whatever He tells you to do that you will humble yourself and trust Him to do the rest!

When we begin to understand what the will of the Lord is for our lives and what assignment He has called us to do, we will grasp sight of what it is that God wants to accomplish by *humbly submitting* to His plans.

The Bible says that Jesus articulately chose these profound and life changing words that converted the hearts of the disciples with this similarity given by saying:

"Whosoever therefore shall humble himself as this little child, the same is the greatest in the kingdom of heaven." **Matthew 18:4**

According to the **NIV** translation this same verse recites:

"Truly I tell you, unless you change and become like little children, you will never enter the kingdom of heaven.

Therefore, whoever takes the lowly position of this child is the greatest in the kingdom of heaven." **Matthew 18:4**

Tell me why do you think little children are ranked as amongst the greatest in the kingdom of heaven?

Is it because they are so pure in heart, that they quickly obey and submit to their parents without controversy or could it be because of their innocent nature, which is of a meek and lowly spirit? or perhaps could there be another valid reason behind this phenomenon that we are unaware of.

"Children are vitally important to God, He honors and esteems them as being gifts that are priceless and valuable treasures to us all."

You see, God chose the weak things of this world to shame the strong. He chose the lowly things of this world and the despised things that are not-to nullify the things that are, so that no one may boast before him.
(See I Corinthians 1:28) **NIV**

Remember how the disciples were bickering amongst themselves as to who was the greatest in the kingdom of God, and later forbade the children to sit on Jesus' lap-this selfish act of inflated pride and arrogance eliminated them from walking in *humility* as modeled by these children.

Jesus was trying to make a point to curtail them from this selfish act by directing their attention solely on the demeanor displayed by the children.

Do you remember how your life was before you accepted Jesus as Lord? To answer that question many of us were men and women trying to live a life without Gods' covenant of emancipation and deliverance.
We, being like many of the disciples were far from being flawless and were by nature born into this world as sinners.

God did not call or choose the disciples based upon their driven performances, nor upon their orientations, achievements, credentials, titles, accolades, ethnicity or gender, but He chose them so that the glory of the Lord could be seen and witnessed by those who did not believe.

As a matter of fact, they were ordinary common men who had real life struggles, real life problems, insecurities, disappointments and failures just as you and I experience in this present life.

Gods' word quickly reminds us that we did not choose Jesus but that He chose and appointed you and I that we might go and bear fruit and that our fruit may be lasting so that whatever we ask the Father in His Name, He may give it to you and I. (See John 15:16)

In the act of rendering service unto The Lord how would you say Jesus views you as being like a little child?

Take careful thought to answering this question to see if your life and actions taken to Gods' admonishment patterns after this next passage below.
As we look to the Gospel of Matthew 23:12 Jesus said:

> **"And whosoever shall exalt himself
> shall be abased and he that shall
> humble himself shall be exalted."**

It is quite evident that Jesus places a considerable amount of emphasis on *humility* and *submission* as a lesson to be both learned and practiced by every believer in our daily affairs by continuous communion with Him in prayer.
This union demonstrates to God that our hearts have become tender to His will-coercing us to be led by His Spirit to obey and move at His command.
Did you know how vitally important it was for Ruth to heed to the command of God during the darkest time in her life?
If you had to make a decision that was predicated on life or death what would you do and who would you turn to for guidance?
Would you like to know Ruth's decision that was made and how she permitted God to intervene on her behalf?
I am so delighted that you do!

  Here we read about a young grieving widow, that was faced with a dilemma who found herself at a crossroad of uncertainty which clouded her decision-making in not knowing which direction to turn to for help.
I am quite confident Ruth felt a myriad of emotions that were expressed in fear, pain, loneliness, distress, grief and shock by the reality of her husband's early death.

In these moving pages, we will read about Ruth's dear mother-in-law, Naomi and come to embrace the great mission she was chosen to do in comforting, guiding and thus, to bring resolution to Ruth's dilemma.

Ruth's close ties that she shared with Naomi proved to be more than just the normal, ordinary, and typical kind of relationship that is shared between a mother-in-law and daughter-in-law.

Naomi was a kind and gentle loving mentor to both of her beloved daughters-in-law and lovingly encouraged, guided and nurtured them even after the deaths of their husbands.

After having suffered the great losses of her husband and her two sons, Naomi experienced some of the very same emotions as Ruth, yet in spite of her very own deep sorrow, Naomi graciously approached her two young daughters-in-law and offered them rest in returning back to Judah.

In her doing so, Naomi had decided that it would be best for her to travel a much different path other than what she had suggested to her daughters-in-law.

Naomi encouraged both of her daughters- in-law to return back to their homelands and decreed Gods' blessings of comfort over their lives prior to departing back to her native land.

As we continue to read this God inspiring story, we will gain insight to some other interesting facts about Ruth and how she operated in the realm of humility.

We will also come to understand the purpose of God's grace on her life and analyze how her childlike approach to submission to God and Naomi which made her testimony praiseworthy and uplifting for us all!

But first, let's give careful attention to the place where God ordained and ordered her steps and the five instructions that were given by Naomi as she tutored and guided Ruth in preparation for the blessings that lied ahead.

To shed more light on their journey, we are told that it was during the late spring when Naomi and Ruth arrived in Bethlehem at the beginning of the barley harvest.

Upon their entrance, the women were greeted by the whole village where close relatives and natives of Naomi's stood eagerly in expressing their excitement and jubilation of her great return.

Once the ladies found a suitable place to live and familiarized themselves in this new territory, I am quite sure that Ruth had become well rested and quite zealous to find work in hopes to show her deep appreciation for all the good that Naomi had done.

The story tells us that one day Ruth approached Naomi to ask if she could go to work in the fields and gather grain behind the plowmen if they would permit her to do so.

Naomi granted Ruth her permission and as she went to glean behind the harvesters she was directed to glean at a precise location of the field that belonged to Boaz.

This wealthy man was a very close relative of Naomi's late husband and is described as being one of the most influential figures in his community, who later on in the story inquires about Ruth and who she was to the harvesters.

Boaz, being the gentleman that he was introduced himself to her and forbade Ruth not to glean behind the men but only behind the women workers.

At the end of a long and tiring day from gleaning in the fields, Ruth returned back to town and told her mother-in-law how much grain she had gathered and that she worked for a man by the name of Boaz.

How do you think Naomi felt when she heard this good news about Ruth gleaning in her deceased husbands' fields? Did Naomi immediately embrace the vision of imagining Boaz and Ruth in the future as being husband and wife?

Do you believe that Naomi heard from the Holy Spirit and submitted to the voice of God to prepare Ruth for the next stage in her life with Boaz?

I believe Naomi heard clearly and by her bold action taken, God also had a blessing waiting in store that was going to cause both she and Ruth's *joy* to be restored and for their mouths to be refilled with laughter once again!

Now that the scene is set, let's move quickly to learn what the first instruction Naomi delegated to Ruth as she prepared her for the expected end.

Please go with me to the book of Ruth beginning at chapter two starting at verse 2 to the place where Ruth is speaking to Naomi and said, "Let me now go to the field, and glean ears of corn after him in whose sight I shall find grace." Notice in this particular verse how Ruth graciously acknowledged Naomi as she sought her permission prior to taking on this task. More than anything Ruth wanted to present herself as a servant to a man whom she had no solid association with, but yet deep in her heart she was convinced that favor would precede her- and it did as we discover later on in the story.

In chapter three we learn the customary method by which Naomi used to secure Ruth's chances of marriage to Boaz that was an eye opener for me as The Holy Spirit gave relevance to these next few passages of scripture.

Naomi was a wise woman who had great hope in God and understood the set time for Ruth's day of Jubilee that was soon to be at hand.

I believe that she executed immediately by faith, taking Ruth by the hand, guiding her step by step, line upon line for what seemed impossible and unending to experiencing God's magnificent possibilities!

The very first instruction that was given to Ruth was:

*To wash, to bathe. This was a sign shown to me by The Holy Spirit as removing any impurities by way of consecration for holy purposes unto God.   **Ruth 3:3**

The second instruction given for Ruth to do was:
*To anoint herself. This was a sign shown to me by The Holy Spirit that symbolized Gods' anointing and favor on Ruth for such a time as this in her life. **Ruth 3:3**
A better way to describe Gods' anointing being displayed in this particular text would be similar to applying, perfume on her wrists[pulse points], that is used basically to amplify the scent, as a means of attraction.

The third instruction recommended for Ruth was:
*To put raiment upon herself. **Ruth 3:3**
The Holy Spirit revealed that this simple act of Ruth putting on fresh and elegant clothing is equated to the believer, adorning him/herself with the royal garments of praise, strength, honor and beauty! (See Isaiah 51:3.)

The fourth instruction that was admonished for Ruth to do was:

*Get thee down to the floor and do not make yourself known. **Ruth 3:3**

This instruction given is similar to the practice of *kneeling* down in a *prostrate position* unto God in the form of worship.

Consequently, this same approach that Ruth was advised to carry out shows us a serious attitude she had in regards to *humility* and *submission*.

As Naomi was led by God's spirit, Ruth was also carefully admonished to use discretion and to lay at the feet of Boaz in a manner which both preserved and protected Ruth's reputation.

The fifth instruction that was given to Ruth was:
*To sit still..." **Ruth 3:18**
This quiet, motionless, silent mode of sitting still after being in the presence of Boaz for Ruth had to be one of the most challenging instructions she was given to do.

Yet because of her respect and trust in Naomi's guidance she quickly obeyed and waited patiently to hear about the outcome of Boaz's meeting with his kinsman.

Similarly, many times after prayer God desires for us to sit quietly in His presence in order that He may speak direct truths into our lives.

In addition, by remaining conscious of His presence guiding us step by step we are able to relax and be still and cease from performing, in knowing that He is God.

Psalm: 46:10 brings us comfort by admonishing us to:

"Be still, and know that I am God."

The sixth instruction given to Ruth not only required for her to be courageous, but it also called for her to be bold and dauntless in order to carry out what Naomi had premeditated.

*When he lies down, that you shall mark the place where he shall lie, and you shall go in, and uncover his feet, and lay thee down, and he will tell you what you shall do."

This mental image that Naomi proposed for Ruth to execute symbolizes and represents the believer's designated place for prayer.

"Where is the designated and marked place you meet God for prayer?"

Could it be that your designated place to meet God is in the very privacy of your home bowing down before Him at your bedside, or outside on your deck as you inhale and exhale the warmth of His tranquil Presence, the guest room perhaps, or maybe it could be in the comfort of your car while driving to work.

It may even be sitting on a bench in the park or dining alone in a private booth at a cozy restaurant.

Just remember no matter where your private place may be always make sure to take time out to talk to God and to include Him in on every facet and minor detail of your life, regardless of how small or how great your concerns may be.

God patiently awaits to hear from you!

The next assignment given to Ruth required her to:
*Remain hidden until Boaz finished dinner and went to sleep and was instructed thereafter to   enter into his lodging quarters.
Some may ask the question, "But why was this particular step so important for Ruth to execute?"

I am so glad that you asked that question.

You see, after Boaz and the other harvesters finished winnowing barley many of them stayed at his place of work from sun up to sun down and would remain there until the very next day.

This action took courage, faith, trust and above all God's grace for Ruth to do such a thing, being that she was the only woman present gleaning the fields that belonged to Boaz.

The question that I would like for you, the reader to ponder over concerning Ruth's obedience is this;

"Do you think that it was appropriate for Ruth to have entered into the living quarters of Boaz's dwelling?"

"If you were in her position would you have second thoughts about carrying out this step?"

Let's explore this charge given to Ruth a little further for just a moment and refine the instructions Naomi strongly advised.

* "Thou shalt go in."

This is another correlation similar to entering into the courts of our God when we are in prayer.

What better way to approach The Father than to be at His footstool and to be able to worship Him with our hands lifted up without wrath, anger or without doubting!

(See Psalm 99: 5, I Timothy 2:8.)

Another instruction that Ruth chose to do out of love and respect for her mother-in-law was:

* "To uncover his feet"...

This course that Naomi gave appears odd and indecent, but it was according to the laws of Israel.

It was customary for widows, such as Ruth to follow this particular rule. When Ruth went to the "threshing floor" where Boaz lodged for the night, she came in secret and delicately removed the [blanket, his own clothing, or perhaps a rug] he used to cover and wrap his feet with for the night.]

This "uncovering" shown to me symbolizes the exposure and revelation of Gods' wisdom- bringing light to unfold the deep unseen mysteries of God's Word that belongs to the believer.

In the book of Deuteronomy 29:29 it decrees:
> "The secret things belong unto the Lord our God, but the things that are revealed belongs to us and to our children forever, that we may do all of the words of this law." **[AMP]**

The very last instruction given by Naomi for Ruth to do was simply to:

* "Lay thee down and he will tell you what you shall do."

We are told that Ruth was not to lie down by Boaz's side, but only to lay *softly* crosswise *at his feet* as the laws and customs of her generation permitted. Ruth was a chaste woman who exemplified great virtue and modesty.

Her loyalty, unfailing commitment, godliness and steadfast confidence she had in Naomi's wisdom prepared her to be a channel of love, which later opened the doors to a wonderful marriage that she shared with Boaz.

In this blessed union, Ruth was able to give birth to a son by the name of Obed, who was the father to Jesse, and Jesse was the father to King David.

From the beginning to the end of this historical love story, we saw how God's plans unfolded in Ruth's favor for the good-in giving her GOD'S very best!

> "Every good gift and every perfect gift is from above, and cometh down from the Father of lights, with whom is no variableness, neither shadow of turning." James 1:17

There is one more special woman that is worthy of mentioning in the Bible that we read about whose name is not given however; her generous act of worship also paints a perfect picture for us to pattern after in our lives.
This illustrious passage that has been recorded in Luke's Gospel beginning in chapter seven gives a human face to this unknown woman whose deed changed the perception and hearts of those that encountered her presence in more ways than one. This is one of those heart-felt stories filled with emotions that will move you to tears and will challenge you to go higher and deeper in your relationship with Jesus. Imagine this setting if you will with me by trying to picture what the atmosphere must have been like when this unknown woman entered the room where Jesus was sitting to have dinner.
As you continue to read this scenario-I am using my own words and imagination to describe this momentous event.

This woman was considered to be a "harlot" and an outcast, that had been labeled by religious heathen as one who did not "fit in" and needless to say, nor was welcomed to be in attendance where Jesus was visiting. However, in spite of their inward and hideous thoughts they perceived towards her, and their negative attitudes displayed, these viewpoints did not intimidate her from entering in the room where Jesus was sitting.

Let's take a look and discover the great impact this woman had specifically on Jesus and those that were present during the dinner.

> "And, behold, a woman in the city, which was a sinner when she knew that Jesus sat at meat in the Pharisee's house, brought an alabaster box of ointment and stood at his feet behind him weeping, and began to wash his feet with tears, and did wipe them with the hairs of her head, and kissed his feet and anointed them with the ointment."
>
> Luke 7:37

Just think with me for a moment how the Pharisees must have felt as they were filled with indignation as she pressed her way courageously to approach Jesus.
Many of them that were present who took notice of her,
I am quite sure murmured in disgust by way of showing discontent and dissatisfaction of her presence in conducting this bold act. Those who witnessed this sacred observance also found it ludicrous in how she had conducted herself, while on the other hand Jesus received her pouring ointment upon His head as a token of honor and worship in the highest respect.

The alabaster box of perfume was most dear and precious to her-so much that she was willing to give it all away to The Savior of the World, The Lamb of God, ***Jesus!***
This woman knew that Jesus was able to cleanse and to wash away her sins.
She understood and did not refrain from giving to Jesus all that she had. Her heart was in the right place and her intentions were pure as she graciously yet quietly knelt down before The King of Kings.

This precious form of *worship* and *submission* in washing the feet of Jesus with her tears and wiping them with the hairs of her head, was indeed a priceless and epic moment for Jesus that took place days prior to His excruciating Crucifixion.

Jesus recognized this as an act of *worship* and *submission* and gave honor to her by blessing her with these piercing words of freedom.

"Thy sins are forgiven."   Luke 7:48
"Thy faith hath saved thee; go in peace.
                                  Luke 7:50

This extraordinary woman left the presence of Jesus with a past that could no longer keep her captive and entered into a new future that yielded peace, joy, dignity, forgiveness, and God's unconditional love!

I want to share another story of two notable sisters in the Bible by the names of Martha and Mary that you might remember when Jesus came to visit one day in their home. This particular narrative in the scriptures demonstrates two types of relationships that God desires for each believer to have-and thus each woman received entirely different results.

As we read the story we will come to understand Martha, the hardworking, industrious and meticulous sister who believed that serving others was the key to her success, while on the other hand we will perceive Mary in a totally different light.
    Mary was the sister who became so enthralled with Jesus' teachings that her focus in assisting Martha as hostess had become less of a priority.

The scriptures plainly signifies that Martha had become quite exasperated, irritated and most annoyed by her sister Mary's action taken to listening to Jesus teachings as opposed to attending to her hostess duties.
Martha continued to take full responsibility of her duties in the household simply because she wanted everything to be just right and done properly.

When Martha failed to gain the attention of her sister's help with serving, the scripture tells us that she outwardly aired such dissatisfaction against Mary by trying to openly embarrass her in front of Jesus and the other guest that were present.

As a matter of fact, the narrative reveals to us that she went to Jesus in seeking His help to intervene and also to rebuke Mary.

The reply Jesus gave to Mary must have been mind boggling for her to receive at first when He said:

"Martha, Martha thou art careful and troubled
about many things: but one thing is needful:
and Mary hath chosen *that good part*, which
shall not be taken away from her." *[Italicized for Emphasis]*

Jesus certainly did not view Martha's serving and being hospitable to others as problematic rather instead, He admonished this kind of service throughout many of His teachings.

On the other hand, He did however take notice of her rude behavior that was directed towards Mary for her lack of attention given to assist her with the guests.

This kind of behavior displayed separated her from the true presence of Jesus.

You see, what she failed to understand was that this "one thing needed" Jesus spoke so gently to her about was the "master key" behind real success regarding Godly and genuine servant-hood. The very moment Martha had decided to put more emphasis on serving the guests rather than listening to Jesus, this action taken quickly became her "downfall."

Remember it was Martha who had invited Jesus and the other guests over to have dinner at her home, and to have behaved so childishly she missed the opportunity to enrich her life with the wisdom that flowed from the very breath of The Father!

"Mary chose the better part, that will not be taken away from her" were the words that Jesus spoke.

She was a woman who plainly understood what true worship was and by no means was she willing to miss an opportunity to have had Jesus right there in her presence and not use this time to receive wisdom that would enhance her spiritually to gaining a closer bond with Jesus.

I like to think of Mary in this regard as it pertains to the passages described so beautifully in Psalm 1 beginning at verse two and three that recites:

"Blessed is the one whose delight is in the law of the Lord, and who meditates on his law day and night."

This person is like a **"tree that is planted by the rivers of water that brings forth his fruit in his season; his leaf shall not wither; and whatsoever he doeth shall prosper."**

As a new follower of Jesus' ministry she planted herself by the "Living Water" **(Jesus)** and eagerly took delight and pleasure in kneeling down at His feet to be taught truths and gain knowledge from His teachings.

We all should strive to be more like Mary in this aspect- dedicated and devoted to spending time each day as we turn our attention by focusing on "the good part, which shall not be taken away."

By making a conscious effort to model after her example it will surely elevate and deepen one's level of love for God that supernaturally exceeds the human depth of love. Unlike Martha, who chose to be consumed with the busyness of putting others first before God, voluntarily dismissed her opportunity to embrace the full richness of Jesus' presence. We all at one time or another in our relationships with God have fallen victim to this prey.

Have you ever stopped to consider: How to have absolute victory over the enemy as you stand firm in your faith to pleasing God rather than man?

The answer submitted to this question is a mere fact that as Christians, we must rather focus on God instead of glorifying "self" which is the enemy to God.

When a believer is set free from the bondage to "self"-he will gain a better understanding and appreciation for what pleases God as he humbly submits to His will.

I am fully convinced from these witnesses we have in the Word of God, that we must first: be of a willing heart and of a willing mind to serve the Lord with joy and gladness. This means that our hearts must be in the right place in order to submit eagerly to the Lord without resistance to His will.

God also gave strict command that we are to submit to those who are in authority over our lives as it is outlined in The King James Version of The Bible in I Peter 5:5 KJV which states:

> **"Likewise ye younger, submit yourselves unto the elder, Yea, all of you be subject one to another, and be clothed with humility for God resists the proud and gives grace to the humble."**

What would happen if all believers would pace and set themselves to follow Jesus' practical footsteps in this call regarding submission?

The answer is given to us in Ephesians 5:1 that says:

> **"Be ye therefore followers of God, as dear children; and walk in love as Christ also hath loved us, and has given Himself for us an offering and sacrifice to God for a sweet smelling savor."**

That clearly means that "we please God by acting in the manner in which He acts".

We are continuously exhorted to be kind to one another as He is towards us, to be forgiving of one another as He has forgiven us, to love one another as He loves us and to submit to one another in the way that He submitted to God, The Father.

In doing so, you begin to supernaturally take on this same behavior of the Divine that has been carefully germinated and delicately cultivated in your heart by the Holy Spirit.

This developed behavior that now flows at will through the life of a true believer can easily be expressed by his/her mannerisms marked with a demeanor that copy the actions of the Father.

This implies that the complete exfoliation or better yet the "stripping" off from our sinful past no longer dominates our moral behavior.

Rather instead, we are now made partakers of the glorious benefits through salvation and by being baptized in Christ by faith, we incorporate a new spiritual life made available through His Spirit, thereby transforming and shaping you and I to morally reflect the very likeness of Him.

A prime example given of this behavior would be similar to how children naturally mimic what they see their parents do and even at times, repeat what they may have heard their parents say, as result of their constant interactions that they have in the home.

The same holds true for the man or woman, boy or girl that will walk circumspectly and closely with God.

The believer who possesses the same mindset as Jesus will be the one that will succumb to *"putting on"* the Christ-like nature of God and soon begin to resemble, mirror, copy and at best to represent Him in the earth!

As you began to acquire to spend adequate time in the Word of God by meditating upon it by day and by night your spirit then becomes automatically alive unto God.

In making this choice, you are literally allowing your witness for Jesus Christ's iridescent, gleaming and blazing bright light that beams in and through you to reflect as a transparent resemblance of Him.

When we submit to His will and securely embrace His Presence, we find great comfort to rest in His promises and are set free to worship The Lord in true holiness, for this is what distinctively resonates to HIM, that we desire to please Him above anything else that this world can offer!

As we come to a close in this chapter I would like to share one more passage that illustriously demonstrate how Jesus made this committed life of *submission* as a daily practice concerning His Divine assignment.
This astounding success to Jesus' ministry is summed up and revealed to us in these last few sentences:

> **"During the days of Jesus' life on earth, He offered up prayers and *petitions* with fervent cries and tears to the one who could save Him from death, and He was heard because of His reverent submission."**   **Hebrews 5:7 NIV**

Let me ask you a question Child of God, "When do you go to God the most?"
Is it a time when you feel that others have failed you and disappointments somehow seem to have forced you into taking a step backwards instead of going forward?
Do you find yourself praying more often when you have fallen short and missed the mark due some of life's compromising and overwhelming, stressful situations?

If this is you, don't become discouraged and despondent, just refocus on Jesus and seek rest in a quiet, unrushed setting where you can hear HIM clearly say these piercing words of tenderness as such…………..

> I LOVE YOU AND NEVER WILL I GIVE UP ON YOU!
> STAY ON COURSE, I AM HERE WITH YOU ALWAYS!
> I WILL ABSOLUTELY, POSITIVELY NOT LET YOU FAIL,
> YOU ARE A WINNER AND A CHAMPION BY MY GRACE!

No matter how big or how small the trial may be to your dilemma, never once forget that your hope is not in Man, your job, your earned money, your status quo or in your circumstances, but in the living God!

As you begin each day to make it a decision of quality by living in His presence and progressively come to know Him more and more, God will undoubtedly, show you His perspective as the Holy Spirit influences and impacts your life-that is lived out in complete obedience unto the Lord!

So with much boldness, I declare over your life that from this day forward that you will seize every opportunity that has been made available by the Holy Spirit to tenaciously by faith, possess and harness these two phenomenal spiritual virtues of *humility* and *submission* that rightfully belongs to you!

"So, what are you waiting for?"

It's time to get on board and get your new start today, right now at this very moment!

*I challenge **you** to gird up **your** strength and to renew **your** mindset to be in agreement with the Word of God.*

*I decree that **you** will be in "hot pursuit" of God, as **you** walk in this new chosen path for **your** life.*

*I decree that **you** will begin to set new goals in hopes by fulfilling them and that **you** will serve the King of Kings and the Lord of Lords in ways greater than **you** have in times past!*   *Amen.*

Chapter 5. *E..* "*Having Great Expectation*"

"My soul wait thou only upon God;
for my expectation is from him."
Psalm 62: verse 5

"Are you in preparation to expect God's very best for your life?" And if so, "What are you doing in preparation to receive His very best that has been designed especially for you?"

From this particular chapter, we will learn and come to understand the importance in taking the first initial steps towards exiting away from being in the spectator's seat of defeat, to uncovering truths from Gods' Word how we are to reposition our postures, attitudes and our outlook, as an active participant towards gaining victory over some of life's most bleak and forbidding circumstances.

Are you familiar with the story in John chapter five that describes an impotent man, who sat beside the pool waiting for the moving of the water in desperate need to be healed?"

The Bible makes mention that this man had been stricken with an infirmity that had kept him bound for thirty-eight long years.

The scripture narrates to us: "That an angel went down at a certain season into the pool, and troubled the water: and whosoever then first after the troubling of the water stepped in was made whole of whatsoever disease he had."

This pool of Bethesda was infamously known to have been a "house of mercy and grace" and was believed by the Jews, that the water in the pool was able to somehow, miraculously heal the sick and those that were afflicted.

This certain man apparently occupied an area there that was close enough by the pool that would enable him to spectate and witness a great multitude of others who were either blind, halted, impotent and weakened, step in aggressively with *having great expectations* to receive their healings.

While on the other hand, because of his passivity and hopelessness-this man had lost all possibilities in dreaming of foreseeing himself as being healed.

In other words, this man remained in a "frozen" position that hindered him from being healed and merely defeated at best.

The question remains; "Was this certain man afraid to commit himself to believing that he too could *expect* to have the very same benefits in receiving his healing as all the others?"

Could it have been that this certain man had become so discouraged, dismayed and somewhat intimidated by the actions displayed by the others jumping into the pool ahead of him that somehow *"crippled his faith"* and *"crushed his confidence?"*

Perhaps none of these observations justified this certain man's circumstance at all.

I can only imagine on that particular day, how excited he must have been to hearing the good news throughout the city, of Jesus' visit to Jerusalem in commemoration of the Jewish feast.

This man may have wondered to himself, if this could be the beginning of a new day for a "golden opportunity" to take place in his life towards being made well.

Please join me as we dive into this passage of scripture in discovering that it matters not how huge, or how minor or how diminutive your problems may be-there is hope in your latter end!

Together, we will pinpoint Gods' sovereign grace that was made evident to a man who didn't know mercy until *Mercy-* who was indeed, **JESUS**-faced and found him!

How many of us know by experience that without God, we can do absolutely nothing!
You see child of God, there was once a time in our lives when we too were without God and without a clue as to Who, He really was!
We were "spiritually dead," and was very much like this certain man in many ways.

For some of us, our spiritual postures resembled his physical disabilities of being *limp* and *lame*.
Having *"no faith"* in God, caused many of us damages to our minds, souls, bodies and in our spirits leaving us with the frail postures into becoming *tilted* and *wilted*.

In some cases, we were like those who had sat by the pool sides that had been afflicted in their physical bodies since birth.
We were blind to sin, weak and impotent in faith, and for those who wrestled with having no faith at all in God, were likened unto a rose bud, fallen to the ground, being separated from its main source, [*the stem*] and left alone, soon to wither away and die!

But because of God's infinite Mercy and His indescribable power of healing and salvation, we can now partake of His grace to live and not die and endeavor to walk in a posture that is *erect* and *correct* to bring honor, beauty and splendor to HIS name!

As we continue to labor in God's word and follow the progress of this certain man's dilemma, we will learn of his success and witness through these pages, the love Jesus has for mankind.

We will also discover by his example how vitally important it was for him to make Jesus to be his main focus rather than on himself and his circumstances.
Isn't it amazing to know, that when we take our eyes off our ourselves and refocus our undivided attention on God, every trouble, fear, worry, frustration, anxiety, problem and difficult situation fades away and ultimately, loses both its power and the grip that it once held on you.

In addition, when we choose to give God first place and choose to make Him our highest priority over every detail in our lives, we quickly come to enjoy life in its fullest as God purposefully intended and to see His Will being accomplished completely in our lives!

God sees every intricate detail in our lives and He never once takes His eyes from off of us.
We are the center of His endless and utmost devoted attention!

The scripture goes on to tell us that Jesus stood from afar and observed this man, signaling him out from amongst the others who sat by the poolside and commanded by the power of God's spoken Word that this man be cured of this tormenting affliction.

What was it about this certain man that made him stand out from amongst all the others?
Have you ever wondered why Jesus' attention was directed towards this certain man as He saw him from afar?

The answer to these questions depicts the Divinity of God and His unfathomable love that He desired for this certain man to come to know.
Jesus saw this man's heart and discerned that he was in need of a Loving Savior.

The ailments of this certain man was obviously witnessed by those who sat near him at the pool, but God in His Infinite wisdom saw the hidden parts to this man's entire being-that others could not see with the human eye.

Do you remember what God said to Samuel when He spoke to him regarding David to be anointed as King? God spoke these words and said:

"….Man looks at the outward appearance but The Lord looks on the heart."

I Samuel 16:7

For one moment, I would like for you to participate with me in an effort to envisioning this man's surroundings; and somehow try to understand the posture Jesus operated in as a result to this certain man's emotional and physical healings and how this certain man must have felt when he finally understood; that he was in the very presence of GOD ALMIGHTY, THE GREAT I AM, JESUS!

There are two powerful scriptures that comes to mind that very well may give answer to these questions.
Follow me very carefully, and if you have access to a Bible please turn to the book of **Romans 8:26-27 [AMP]** and read during your quiet time the 139th division in the book of Psalm.

Do you have your Bibles open to read these two powerful scriptures? If so, let every ear hear and every heart receive what God's Word teaches us as to what may be a "possible" answer in how this certain man may have felt on the day of his unexpected miracle.
The apostle, Paul speaks eloquently about the role and personality of The Holy Spirit and gives us a glimpse of how God's Divine intervention to our prayers are received and how it is He, Who intercedes on our behalf when we are unable to pray as we should.

I believe that this next passage we are about to study perfectly describes the heart and the soul of the certain man's silent cry out to God and as you read its contents, begin to see yourself when you are at the breaking point in your life, pleading for the mercies of God to console and heal all of your wounds. And the scripture reads:

So too, The Holy Spirit comes to our aid and bears us up in our weakness; for we do not know what prayer to offer nor how to offer it worthily as we ought, but the Spirit Himself goes to meet our supplication and pleads in our behalf with unspeakable yearnings and groanings too deep for utterance. verse. 26

And He Who searches the hearts of men knows what is in the mind of the Holy Spirit what His intent is, because the Spirit intercedes and pleads before God in behalf of the saints according to and in harmony with God's will. verse. 27

Religion would have us to believe that in order to get something from God, we must first do something that requires the believer to put forth effort by performance to obtain Gods' blessing.

Not necessarily so in the case of this story or any part of the Gospel of Grace. Praise God!

In observance of Jesus' words spoken directly to this certain man, **"To rise and take up thy bed and walk,"** notice that this man never once asked, nor thought or did anything so noticeable in performing to get Jesus' attention to heal him.

The Bible declares that **for by "grace" are ye saved through faith; and that not of yourselves: it is a gift of God: not of works, lest any man shall boast."**

Ephesians 2:8-9

Gods' compassionate *grace* that never ceases, was the only hope for this certain man's deliverance in gaining his healing both physically as well as spiritually.

This man never claimed to have known Jesus according to the writings of John nor does it reveal if he was a man of faith or not.

Regardless of this man's dismal situation that seemed to have per say, "incarcerated" him in the *spectator's seat*, Gods' Divine purpose was designed to free him from the dark and negative influences that had kept him bound.

This was simply a test that God allowed by permitting this man to pass. You see, God is on our side and never tests us for our own defeat- but the test is given to show us that our strength is in Him and that we are more than conquerors through Him that loves us.

(See Romans 8:37) **KJV**

Another connotation of this mindset is quoted in the twenty-fourth division of Psalm verse 16 that reads:

**"For though the righteous fall seven times,
they rise again, but the wicked stumble when
calamity strikes."** **NIV**

The adversary, the devil oftentimes will try to allure us into regressing back to our old carnal ways of living in sin and sadly to say, some do err-only to find themselves once again, to be enslaved by the temptation and easily *snared in his set traps, becoming the prisoner and the victim to sin.*

But you can be assured child of God, that it's not how many times that a righteous man falls down, but it is simply how many times that a righteous man gets up and retains his faith in God to continue the journey!

In this next scenario, we will embark on a spiritual principle that is communicated by means of presenting a common analogy, in an effort to what I believe will assist to clarify the true essence of the wicked tactics of the enemy.

If you were born between the years of 1940-1960 this scenario will probably bring back fond memories and hopefully will better help us to visualize how Satan attempts to allure and entrap us into a life of bondage and despair.

One fond memory that I can recall growing up was overhearing my parents discussing a plan in how they could trap a mice that apparently had made our attic, its home. How many of us know that having a rodent in your home is not good, at least in our home it was totally out of the question!

Do you remember the old-fashioned in home wooden snap mouse traps that you could purchase at your local indoor/outdoor home improvement store?

My parents had decided that this would be their best option to try in preventing lesser activity of the rats from re-occurring.

This assembly usually came with a metal bait wire trigger and the U-shaped metal bar and the metal pin that typically would fit into a slot near the bait trigger.

My father normally would set the trap where he would see traces and signs of the mouse, and later, not to fail to mention, the most important thing, *"the bait."*

The bait that he used at times was either cheese, peanut butter, or an attractant gel. We all understand the science behind this great invention and how it works.

Once the mouse notices the cheese or the peanut butter placed on the pin, the rat becomes *charmed*, you might use as a better term, and begins to investigate in finding a way to eat the bait without getting trapped or terminated!

A Word to the Wise..... Take heed and be sure not to allow Satan to allure, tempt and trap you with the old "baits" of your past!

Now let us turn our attention once more to the conditions of this certain man's challenges that Satan used in an attempt to contain this man in living a life of misery, pain and defeat. The pains, the trials, and the tribulations that encased this certain man must have been tormenting throughout those thirty-eight years of his life.

The scripture does not specifically mention how many times he was taken to the pool but we do know that he was in the right place at the right time on the day he was summoned to get up.

God graciously demonstrated His love and healing virtue towards this particular man so that his faith could be exercised, strengthened and expanded for the glory of God.

The very moment that the impotent man answered Jesus' first question directed to him, *"Wilt thou be made whole?"* [*Italicized for Emphasis*] he responded sadly with a tone of loneliness as having no close relationship with anyone to care for him that resonated a message of self-pity, gloom, despondency and mere hopelessness.

Yet, when the words of Jesus was released for the second time in commanding him to take his rightful position to rise and take up his bed and walk which transitioned him as now being *a participator (the energetic, vigorous, aggressive one)* he immediately was made whole, took up his bed and walked!

The record tells us that afterwards Jesus found this man in the temple and said unto him, **"Behold, thou art made whole: sin no more, lest a worse thing come to you"** and the man departed and told the Jews that it was Jesus, which had made him whole.   **John 5:14-15**
[Italicized for Emphasis]

We can now interpret from this story that this certain man's entire life had changed for the better.

His life would never be the same again, because of his direct contact in being in the very Presence of The only One that could have healed him and loved him more than he could have ever loved himself!
This man's conversion led him to such crystalized depths of repentance, boldness and a life of emancipated freedom!

Child of God, it is when we believe on the name of The Lord Jesus and voluntarily offer our lives, our plans and our will to Him that all things are made new that clears the path to a satisfied life of obedience and a promising destiny!

Allow this certain man's measure of faith to be an example to us that God is the God of all flesh and that He is longsuffering to us, not willing that any should perish, but that all should come to repentance.   (See II Peter 3:9.)

There is never any circumstance in your life that that God does not see or any place too dark or so desolate that He cannot find you!

God not only sees you at all times; but He sees you as the righteousness of God in Christ Jesus as His redeemed.
"Did you know that having great *expectation* along with having a *prepared heart* are the very foundational keys that unfolds and unlocks the doors to unanswered prayers?"
Think about it, for without *preparation* there cannot be an *expectation* or better yet said, when *expectation* is not present or activated in a believer's life it hinders and suffocates that desired thing from coming to pass.
These two most powerful components that have been given to activate our faith are in essence, I believe to be the "chief promoters" in obtaining the gift of God's promises.

They have been given to teach us two essential things:

To Trust and To Believe God!

God desires to give each of us life more abundantly that is not necessarily predicated solely on the physical aspect but to give to us life eternally as well.

The same statement held true for this certain man.

Gods' sovereign grace reached out to this man by asking him to do something that he had never did before in his life and that was to step outside of the parameters that he was accustomed. By doing so, his life changed for the better!

Beloved, always know that God will never ask you to do something that He is not willing to do Himself as it pertains to your covenant you have with Him!

For instance, just as He gently commanded and compelled this man to make a choice to pick up his bed and walk; Jesus, also had to follow His Father's command to lay down His life as a living sacrifice so that you and I would be acquitted through His very own blood.

As Jesus' assignment came to an end here on earth, He spoke these very last words by saying, **"It is finished."**

The time has come for you beloved, to believe and to receive by faith and not by your own merits to partake of all of the provisions of the "finished works" Jesus has already made available for you to enjoy as His precious sons and daughters!

So, let your faith resound loudly and abide in His presence as you grow to understand His unmerited grace, the height, width and length of His unconditional love He has for you!

The moment you began to behold and embrace His immeasurable love, there can be nothing that will be able to stop or prevent you from fulfilling your divine purpose on this earth!

For the remaining part of this chapter we will learn why it is necessarily vital for the true believer to develop a *living faith* in God.

This *"living faith"* is the lethal weapon that every believer must exercise to become proficient to step away from a spectator's corner to enter into a participator's arena in living the good, wholesome, prosperous and victorious life. I don't know about you, but I choose to believe God and His immutable Word, regardless of what comes my way by purposefully making it my aim to live a life of faith-no matter what!

The epistle James said something quite interesting in the book of James 2:26 who expressively made this statement:

"For as the body without the spirit is dead,
so faith without works is dead also."

What was James saying and how did this certain man's state of being resemble this last phrase to this passage of scripture?

Let's move on and discover how it correlates with this story.

I would like to propose to you that this parallel signifies "a life lived without faith is likened to a dead corpse, a body without a soul."

Let's paint this picture by using this visual equation to simplify this statement just made.

NO FAITH + NO WORKS = DEAD FAITH

The reciprocal of this visual equation would be:
"A life that is lived out *with* faith is likened
unto a man that *believes in God to* **Do** what
he (Man) is unable to do on his own.

LIFE OF FAITH + TRANSFORMING POWER = LIVING FAITH

Now the question remains, "Why is faith without works dead?"

The epistle James was not saying that it is through our works that make us righteous before God or our efforts or by good performances that gives justification to our redemption through the blood of Jesus unto salvation.
But, what the scripture clearly does say is that a life of faith, saved by grace will result in the transforming power of the nature of a true believer's spiritual heart condition that reveals what he earnestly believes-that is both seen and witnessed by others.

Follow me very closely as we gain insight to learn the true meaning of this statement that is sometimes taken out of context as it can mislead some to believe that it is our *works* and *performances* that create salvation.

Remember when Jesus said, **"Be it unto you according to your faith,"** He was figuratively saying that you and I were created as free moral agents and given a free will to choose and to decide what we will receive through His Written (Logos) Word or through God's Spoken (Rhema) Word, according to your *earnest expectation of faith.*

The *Earnest expectation* I am referring to can be defined as the state of an individual's inner thoughts that expresses an intense eagerness in hopes for some good thing or event in their lives to occur or come to pass.
A perfect example given to describe this definition would the enthusiasm and eagerness that is associated between the proud parents-to-be of a newborn baby.
Another simplistic example to help clarify our *earnest expectation*-could be the jubilant anticipation of Jesus's return.
For some, it may be the *earnest expectation* of desiring physical healing in ones' body or perhaps it could be an undernourished child that prays to God daily to send Christian missionaries to their country to provide food and shelter for his sustainment to live.

Whatever the event-whatever the circumstance or state of affairs may be, Gods' desire is for every believer to believe on Him with having an *earnest expectation* that He will do exactly what He says that He will do!

Did you know that **Ephesians 3:20** confirms this very statement.

Paul attest this truth by saying; **"Now unto Him that is able to do exceeding abundantly above all that we ask or think, according to the power that work in us."**

The ultimate way to maintain this spiritual virtue to our *earnest expectation* of faith, the believer must firmly stand in God's great grace (by not trying to earn His blessings by works) and be willing to spend an adequate amount of quality time in the Word of God.

A true believer can find complete security and relief in the comfort of knowing that a life lived close to God is a life that is sure to constantly, consistently yield His resolute abundance, wisdom, joy, love, richness and continuing presence.

A true believer, whose heart is filled and nourished
with an abundance of living faith becomes
the attractant to where
Gods' glory and His radiance glows!

Matthew's gospel encourages us with this promise:

> **"But seek ye first the kingdom of God, and His righteousness; and all these things will be added unto you."** **Matthew 6:33**

On the contrary, the life of a believer that does not yield to God by meditating on His Word daily can result to a life of emptiness, hopelessness, ignorance and defeat.

God said in His word; **"My people perish for a lack of knowledge…"** and you must not allow yourself to become prey and fall victim to this type of stimuli.

(See Hosea 4:6.)

God desires to infuse our minds with His words, as a means to give life to our spirit that breeds true living faith.
We are to attend to His words and incline our ears to His sayings.
The most important thing is to not let them depart from our eyes and to keep them in the midst of our hearts.

(See Proverbs 4:20-21.)

How many of us have heard this bitter truth before?

"You can't take out what you did not put in!"

No Deposit = No Withdrawals.

My beloved grandfather had even a better way of expressing this phrase by saying;

"Nothing-from Nothing-leaves-Nothing!"

A perfect illustration of this saying is analogous to what happens in the event when the monetary funds in your account has been overdrawn and depleted from your bank account. Maybe you've had this awkward and unfortunate experience to happen to you.

This compromising and uncomfortable situation can easily affect you in several ways.

In most case scenarios, an overdraft protection service is offered that will allow the account holder to temporarily make purchases. However, don't be alarmed when you receive your bank statement in the mail and find that charges were applied for your indiscretion.

Similarly, this scenario reminds me of what happens to the believer when we neglect and put aside precious time that is not shared with God the Father.

"Have you ever experienced those unpredictable times in life when we find ourselves in a tough predicament that demands God's attention, and it seems as though God is not near and that your prayers for some odd reason just seems to go unanswered?"

If you have found yourself in this temporary position, invite God to be involved in every facet of your life.

The good news my friend is taking comfort in knowing that God is your strength in the times of trouble. When we run to Him and abide in His presence we are guaranteed absolutely safety from all seen and hidden dangers.

The Bible recurrently reminds us at all costs to always:

> **"Trust in Him at all times, you people;**
> **pour out your hearts to Him, for God**
> **is our refuge." Psalm 62:8 NIV**

One of the constant testimonies I have both heard and witnessed my Pastor say over the years that has inspired and brought consolation to me was this insightful truth and I quote: "If believer's would make it their common practice of staying in the face of God, they will never have to worry about getting what is in His hands!

As Christians, our deliberate priority should first and most importantly, be to animatedly pursue and seek God by making Him our First Love.

How many of us know that if our priorities are not in the right places and our hearts are not in tune with God and following pursuit with keeping His Word, more than likely you are living a life of imbalance. We are to put Him first above all things, including our relationships that we have with our spouses, our children, our church, our jobs, and even our personal professional goals and objectives.

Unfortunately, there will still be some people who will in fact strongly oppose to this frame of thinking.

These are they who are consumed with their own selfish motives and agendas and have not yet, totally submitted their lives to God!

As we mentioned previously, God should be above all things that takes place in our lives: whether big or small.

To easily avoid falling in the "mundane" of constantly being on the go in meeting other demands of your day, know that God is hovering over you with a desire to instruct and teach you in the way you should go.

I must admit, the more time I spend studying His Word, talking openly to the Holy Spirit as I would with a close friend and pray, the closer I am to Him and the closer I believe that He is to me! For me, life doesn't get any better than that!

Your sacrifice of time spent alone in the presence of The Lord should never be looked upon as being mysterious or a menial task, but an empowerment that brings joy both to you and to God!

The Lord desires for us to taste and see that He is good and to trust in Him at all times. (See Psalm 34:8.)
Let's engage in another story about a crippled man that did not allow his infirmity to interrupt his *earnest expectation* of faith to being healed that has been recorded in the book of Acts 3:1-8.
According to this narration, we are told that both Peter and John were going up to the temple to pray and worship and as they arrived there sat a man that was crippled from birth.
The story tells us also that this the crippled man was carried and laid daily at the gate called "Beautiful" to beg for money from those who were entering in the Temple to worship and to pray.

On this particular day Peter and John arrived to enter the Temple, the crippled beggar asked them for money.
Peter looked at the man and together with John, declared by saying to the man, "Look on us."
The man responded happily, expecting to receive coins from them but instead, Peter declined his request and stood up to the man with authority and said, "silver and gold have I none, but such as I have, give I thee."

Having heard such a charge as this, I imagine that this man had become somewhat disappointed, saddened and feeling totally rejected.

But immediately after Peter spoke these words he declared and decreed over this man with these power impacted words: "In the name of Jesus Christ of Nazareth rise up and walk."

This crippled man instantaneously acted in faith as Peter took him by the hand and lifted him up to his feet.

By his simple act of obedience the story tells us his feet and ankle bones received strength and that he leaped, stood up and walked into the Temple praising God!

This man's great leap of faith that was mixed with such an untarnished *expectation* to being healed, freed him from the entanglements of living a life that had been mingled with doubt, fear and unbelief.

I believe this bold act to his faith demonstrated, was indeed the link that connected him to Peter and John's anointing-which bridged the way to joining him to the great and magnificent power to God's anointing and favor as the result to his divine healing.

I imagine every "baby step of faith" that was taken by this man in collaboration with God, rightfully justified and qualified him as the recipient to this creative miracle in receiving God's richest blessings!

The countless times that this man must have sat at the Gate called "Beautiful" demonstrates his free will, his hope, and perseverance in obtaining the physical manifestation to his healing!

His high level of *expectation* escorted him to the beginning of living a lifelong abundant life that poured profusely from the throne of God's Grace, having with it the supremacy to save him, and to deliver him from a life of deep despair and misery!

Remember, *"Without faith it is impossible to please God."*
(See Hebrews 11:6.)

This man's expectation that he embraced in receiving the manifestation to his miraculous healing, substantiates living proof that a life that is lived by faith to trust God and to depend on God is without doubt, is precisely what pleases God!

Do you recall the question that I asked at the beginning of this chapter?

The question was, "What are you doing in preparation to expect Gods' very best for your life?" What was your answer? "Would it be true to confirm that your reply to this question is; **Yes**, I am prepared to totally trust and believe God to bring every Promise to fruition into my life or perhaps could it be the other way around.

Maybe it could be a particular circumstance or something that took place in your past that have caused you to doubt and not fully believe.

Whatever the situation-whatever the case may be,
God longs for you to trust in Him.

The times in your life when you feel as though everything is out of control, began to lift up your hands to God, and thank Him for your way out to victory!

By complying in giving thanks to Him, these supernatural responses will confuse, stifle, and paralyze this attitude that tries over and over again to control you from trusting and believing God. You must learn how to thank God for everything, although your emotions may try to lead and persuade you to do something entirely different, call on the name of The Lord, Jesus and begin to affirm your trust in Him, no matter how you feel.

God soberly implores us in **I Thessalonians 5:18** that we should be filled with thanksgiving to the fulfillment of God's will that our prayers are being heard.

"In everything give thanks for this is the will of God in Christ Jesus concerning you."

As you begin to take each step to the *preparation* stages of receiving God's very best, ask The Holy Spirit to assist you to go forward when you feel the temptation to doubt.

Remember, The glory of God's Spirit dwells within you
and He is nearer than you think
to help guide and direct your steps.

So let your voice be heard and serve notice on the enemy that your "Days of doubt" are finally over and now since you have decided to let God arise over your emotions, it is now time for your enemies of (doubt and unbelief) to be scattered and buried, never to rise again! (See Psalm 68:1.) So rejoice and be exceedingly glad that God is on your side and that He is prepared to bring His Promises to fruition in your life!

As you continue to surround yourself in the constancy of The Father's unshakable and steadfast love you will come to understand how amazing God really is!

In your time of fellowship you will become even more amazed as you begin to see yourself operating in the spirit of love.

The more contact you have with The Lord, the more of a blessing you become to others by spreading the love of Jesus into their lives.

The world is waiting on *you* to show them God's love and that is why it is so vitally important, to know that God loves you.

To not understand this love, your witness becomes less effective in the lives of others as it should be where God's love is concerned!

You know, it's one thing to be able to motivate people when they need encouragement or stroke their "ego" by inflating their heads with nonsense and not speaking the truth in love.

But, when a true believer, who is confident in God's love crosses the paths of individuals whose lives are turned upside-down, where confusion and turmoil somehow seemed to have governed their minds, that is the time when a believer's *light of God's love* should be shown and the moment for the *light of God's love in you and through you should shine its brightest!*

Just think, their lives will never ever be the same again because you showed up! Glory be to God!

Did you know on the day you accepted Jesus into your heart that you were supernaturally filled with the divine floodgate of His Spirit of Love? "Christ in you the hope of his glory." (See Galatians 5:23, Colossians 1:27.) This agape love, unlike any other love is not to be easily compared to the world's type of love.

As a matter of fact, God's agape love on the inside of a believer is actually what separates you from those who are in opposition with God.

The wonderful reality of it all, is that you don't have to perform to earn God's love, it's automatic on God's part to love you in spite of your shortcomings, idiosyncrasies, sins and failures.

In fact, if that was the case and we all had to perform to gain His love-needless to say, we all would be doomed and sentenced to a life of eternal damnation.

(See 1 Peter 3:18.)

God's love is a free gift that cannot be brought or sold. This free gift of God's love given to humanity is amplified when it is received by faith and is esteemed to be the "most" genuine and greatest gift ever-given from The Lord to His children!

It is most comforting to know that while you and I were sinners-**[Brackets Mine] [people without a covenant with God]** that God still commended His love towards us and yet He died on the cross and shed His blood so that we would be saved from wrath. (See Romans 5:8.)

This unconditional, everlasting, unwavering, and never ending manner of love that God has bestowed upon us grants us the privilege and the highest honor to be called the sons and daughters of The Most High!
(See I John 3:1.)

In light of all that has been laid before you, it is my hope my friend, that you will come to know that God is forever, eternally committed to loving you! There is absolutely nothing that you can do to stop or prevent HIM from loving you!
God Loves You...Yes You!

God's Word solemnly assures us with the answer as to why He is so committed to you and I as noted in these next few lyrics that has been chronicled in I John 4:9-10.

> **"In this was manifested the love of God
> towards us, because that God sent his
> only begotten son into the world, that
> we might live through him.
> Herein is love, not that we loved God,
> but that He loved us, and sent his Son
> to be the propitiation for our sins."**

*We have a guaranteed word of promise that God's love cannot
be broken or shaken, a promise that God loves you
with all of His heart, His soul,
His mind and His strength.*

> **What shall we say to these things?**
> **Who shall separate us from the love**
> **of Christ? Neither height, nor depth,**
> **nor any other creature, shall be able**
> **to separate us from the love of God**
> **which is in Christ Jesus our Lord.**
> **Romans 8:31, 35, 39**

Bear in mind, if you are having challenges in believing the vast love God has for YOU, I I humbly ask that you would take this time to pry your attention away from the burdensome challenges, problems and cares in your life and began to open your heart and your mind to *accept*, to *believe* and to *receive* the full portion of *God's love*.

Take into account, every step of your walk with God will require an act of faith, valor, fearlessness, and boldness in overcoming these cares.

So I encourage you to faithfully **T**rust God, **W**alk in His love, **L**ive to love, **T**urn your attention to Him, **S**it quietly in His Presence, **L**isten to Him, **R**est in the assurance of His love and let Him **P**our into your vessel the extravagant contents of His love, peace and joy!

Take a moment and ask the Holy Spirit to assist you with these gestures and then ask Him to show you how to *open* and *offer* your heart to Him so that you can become like a "tributary" of His love that flows freely and fluently into the lives of others.

So tell me, do you now realize how significant your life is to God? Did you know that He has a design (tattoo) of you on the palms of His hands and that you are the focal point of His undivided attention? (See Isaiah 49:16.)

Are you aware of the rightful purpose of God's plan for your life? Do you know that you are the apple of God's eye? (Deuteronomy 32:10.)

Did you know the emphasis placed on God's vast capacity to loving you is far greater than your faith and it exceeds by endless boundaries of your *earnest expectations* and hope, according to I Corinthians 13:13?
Do you know you are like a precious gem to Him and in His eyes you are valuable, priceless and above all dearest to Him? Did you know because of God's great love that He has for you that He will never deprive or ever with-hold His very best from you?

Just for the record, God will never grow out of love with you
nor will the love that He has for you vacillate or die.
His love for you never pauses, not for one split second,
It is Everlasting!

God's greatest desire is to give you His very best that He has to offer in every area of your life.

Our Heavenly Father's very best gifts given to you are simply characterized in many facets through the gift of praise, thanksgiving, joy, peace, His Holy Spirit, healing, laughter, wholesome relationships, protection, soundness of mind, prosperity, success, strength and the list goes on and on.

God takes great delight to give you the very best by placing it into the hands of His anointed vessels-Yours!

To not accept, believe or to receive this truth about God's Divine and undeviating nature would be like a "cold slap in His face."
This type of attitude implies that God would have to deny Himself as being *Love, Who is Love* and we know, that God could never swear by anything or anyone greater than Himself, because *He is the Way, The Truth and The Life and God is love.*
[Italicized for Emphasis] (See John 14:6, Hebrews 6:13.)

By allowing yourself to dismiss or to forget how God desires to give you the very best, you become an easy target for the archenemy Satan, to manipulate and to monopolize you in living a life of defeat and mediocrity.
So rather than accept this untruth from the enemy, we are admonished to "fight the good fight of faith."

The Bible also gives us another excellent instruction that we are to determinedly resist the devil and he will flee at the beckoning of giving voice to Gods' word.
(See James 4:7 KJV.)

We are also admonished to declare God's Word wisely and seek the guidance of the Holy Spirit to help to guard our hearts with all diligence as we keep His perspective in mind.

"There is no substitute that can or will ever take the place of God's Word."

By "confessing" His Word- meaning *(to declare out loud)* on a daily basis, you will embark on a new way of thinking and develop an assuredness in your spiritual walk, that, in turn, will transform you inside out- all for the glory of God!
So let God be at work in you today by feasting on these confessions of His promises and watch your progress flourish into these Godly amazing results!

"God so loved**[Brackets Mine] [Put your name here]** that He gave His only begotten son so that **[Put your name here]** would not perish but that **[Your name here]** would have everlasting life."   (See John 3:16)

I,[Put your name here] am confident, that God's love for me is mighty, and He will rejoice over me with joy; He will rest in His love and He will joy over me with singing.
(See Zephaniah 3:17)

God loves **[Put your name here]** so much that, He fearfully and wonderfully created and fashioned me to be just like Him, **I,[Put your name here]** am His child and accepted as His Beloved. (See Psalm 139:14)
(See Ephesians 1:6)

God has called you to live in perfect peace and to walk each day trusting dependently on Him with confidence and sure-footedness in knowing that God loves you unconditionally!
Allow this very next passage of scripture to become a part of your daily lifestyle and watch God do mightily on your behalf!

> **"Be strong and very courageous, be careful to obey all the law my servant Moses gave you; do not turn from it to the right or to the left, that you may be successful wherever you go. Keep this book of the Law always on your lip; meditate on it day and night, so that you may be careful to do everything written in it then you will be prosperous and successful."** **Joshua 1:7-8 NIV**

God's purposeful plan is for you to always win and never ever to fail. "Do you believe that?"

If you answered "yes" to this question begin to ask God to lead you in the direction of His holy calling and His perfect choosing for your life.

If you find yourself doubting any of these questions that were presented earlier throughout this chapter, I kindly would like to suggest that you express to God how you feel and ask Him to shed light and expose every dark lie that you have believed.

There is a prophecy which in fact has been traced back in the Old Testament that gives to you and I the advantage over the enemy in his maneuvers to try to deceive us-and this promise is located in the book of **Deuteronomy 29:29** which reads:

> **"The secret things belongs unto the Lord our God: But those things which are revealed belong unto us: and to our children forever, that we may do all the words of this law."**

Child of God, once your eyes have been enlightened to the truth of God's word in discovering that He desires to give you the very best- just remember to keep your mind stayed on Him and foremost, be determined to live in the glorious light of His Presence-the secret place where you are gradually transformed from glory to glory in detecting His great love for you.

This type of awareness in your love walk will positively undoubtedly increase your ability in living a life to expose God's objective by helping you to focus on the abundant life that God has *prepared* in advance for you.

Come take a stroll with me as we closely observe in the finale of this chapter to one of the most magnificent visions of God's Master Plan in the arena of *"preparation"* for Adam and Eve.

We unreservedly understand that God designed, and with careful intent created with purpose The Garden of Eden *in advance* prior to the creation of Adam and Eve to be their safe haven and the secret dwelling place for their new home.
This new place called "home" embodied for them the complete satisfaction, delight and enjoyment to where they found comfort, protection, and love from God.

This luxurious garden is described to us in The Bible to be a place that was fenced in with herbs and trees that were fit for food and more beautiful than anyone could have ever imagined.

According to the Old Testament, Eden symbolized a place where things grew, flourished and was the life form for grass, foliage, shrubbery, fruits, farm-produced goods such as grains, meats, oats, berries of all sorts, underwater seas and rivers that gave character to all vegetation types.

Many Bible scholars have spiritually defined Eden as being a place that represented "unbroken fellowship."

This Garden was indeed believed to be both beautiful and lavish, yet, it also symbolized and represented something even more amazing-it was distinctively created as a sacred place for "lasting relationships" and "unbroken fellowship" to evolve and carefully be developed between God, Adam and Eve.

Did you know that one of God's greatest desires was to have a family ?

Adam and Eve were not just placed in the Garden to be at leisure 24 hours a day, nor to eat themselves in oblivion, sleep and roam throughout the Garden all day long without having any responsibilities, but they were given commands by God to royally exercise their absolute rule, dominion and authority over every living creature and over all the earth and to take special care of the Garden.

This luxurious Garden, that had been meticulously and most uniquely hand-crafted and architecturally designed by God was an extraordinary ingenuous artwork that only He could have majestically *pre-arranged, made ready* and *planned* well ahead in advance for them.

This would of course be the "secret dwelling place" of Adam and Eve's new home-a place of great abundance and love, a place of abode to where God provides His riches in glory that He might show to Adam and Eve His surpassing riches of his grace and kindness towards them.
(See Psalm 91:1, Philippians 4:19, Ephesians 2:4-7.)

The Word of God shines brightly from the words of Paul in the segment of Philippians 1:6 that justify God's intent for the assignment He has called every true believer to fulfill with this assuring verse found in Philippians 1:6.

"Being confident of this very thing, that He which hath begun a *good work in you will perform it* until the day of Jesus Christ." [*Italicized for Emphasis*]

This good work given to Adam to *tend* and *keep* the Garden was the new beginning of Adam's training into becoming what I would like to call-The Entrepreneur, CEO, CFO, Business Managing Partner, Industrialist, Investor, and also as Co-Chairman of the Garden.
Daily, as God shined the light of His glorious Presence into Adam's life, moment by moment, he began to operate proficiently in a manner which mimicked and ultimately complimented God, The Father.

Adam's ongoing constant meetings alone with God most certainly prepared him for the goal that was at hand.
By strategically being placed in this preserved and sufficient environment, Adam was given the opportunity and the privilege to experience what it was like to live in perfection and to enjoy God's very best for his life!

A question comes to mind, "Could there have possibly been something in particular that God had purposely left undone in the Garden of Eden?"

Absolutely not, but if He did, "Have you ever wondered why God charged both Adam and Eve to dress and tend to the Garden?"

We have determined that all of the plants, the trees, and rivers that moistened the Garden properly for vegetation was indeed manufacturing so perfectly that Adam and Eve had no wants in lacking anything that they could have ever thought of that God had already *prepared* for them.

However, there still remains that pending question as to why God gave this command?

There are many wonderful spiritual and natural lessons to be learned here, so without further inquiry let's probe this story as we unfold this great mystery.

Very simply, it is quite clear to understand God's perfect intent in the role Adam was to play in the Garden of Eden.

Firstly, God placed Adam in the Garden to be a living functional, equal partner with The Holy Trinity and most importantly, to be an effective participant with Him in overseeing the property to which he was commissioned to supervise.

Adam was in fact made to be a steward over God's property. He had been graced with The God's wisdom and knowledge, having the supernatural ability to do the following: To *manage* God's resources in the Garden, to *preserve* its beauty, watch over it, *protect* it, to *guard the garden* and to *exercise* diligently what God had placed in his hands; the *dominion* and *authority* to *rule* and *reign* and to *replenish* the earth.

Adam and Eve's responsibility assigned to them may have appeared to be small in our eyes, but in God's eyes, it was seen as them taking charge and acting in obedience that demonstrated respect and reverence towards Him.

Adam and Eve had a choice to make and they chose to obey God in this area by accessing their will to be in total compliance with executing God's spoken command.
Tell me, "Have you ever taken the time to think about the many sacrifices of the limitless measures your parents took to prepare for your future?"
As you sit back and read my short testimony in the next few paragraphs, I want you to reflect on one positive childhood memory that inspires you the most to see how God majestically *prearranged, prepared and planned ahead* in advance about every intricate detail that concerns you.

Please follow me carefully, as I began to mildly stroke and paint this transparent picture of a tender moment in time during my early childhood days.

For you see, it all started with God, The Father who supernaturally empowered my parents with wisdom as He equipped them for a journey that required them "to walk by faith and not by sight."
My parents were very young when they married and did not know exactly all of the twists, directions, and turns of their journey but what they did know was this one thing; and that was to rely completely on God together as their Heavenly Father, to be the Navigator and the Planner of their future.
"For I know the plans I have for you, declares the Lord, plans to prosper you and not to harm you, plans to give you hope and a future." [*Italicized for Emphasis*]   Jeremiah 29:11

Together as one, they trusted this prophetic Word from God and allowed Him to *prepare* the way that brought them to a certain place- where I still call "*home*" today.
In the Porter household, it was no strange mystery or uncommon thing for both our parents to assign chores to the each of us to do around the house.

In fact, there was always one specific duty that we were expected to do on a daily basis, and that was to keep our bedrooms tidy as a way of *dressing* or you might even say to *keeping* them in order.

Looking back in time, I can distinctly hear my beloved Mother's exact firm words as she counseled us by saying; *"Your Father and I have worked together as one by providing you all a good, loving, clean and comfortable home to live in and what we expect from you is to take care of it with a sense of dignity, and honor."*

As a youngster, I didn't fully understand the concept and the entire meaning of what my parents were teaching me at the time. But what I did come to fully comprehend and understand through my training were the essential disciplines to obedience, respect, diligence, stewardship, responsibility, and the principles of walking in humility.

"My learning is simply an unending voyage that sets sail to the acquisitions in expanding the application of my experiences in life."

"What then shall we say would be God's lesson for Adam to learn from his training-by taking care of his home in *the Garden?*"

My thoughts to this question is one that would have me to believe that it was God's profound and distinct pleasure to have ordained Adam to represent Him in the earth, resembling Him in authority as the caretaker of the Garden.

At this moment I kindly invite you to take out your journal and began to jot down some insights God desires to share with you.

As you ponder on this thought, ask the Holy Spirit to reveal the hidden things that you know not of as you sit quietly at His feet and *learn* of Him.

I challenge you to incorporate this practice on a daily basis in your fellowship with God and as you begin to do so- expect to witness a revolutionary, transformation to take place in your life.

When you begin to grasp the full understanding of God's purpose in training Adam to *dress* and *keep* the Garden, you will quickly come to acknowledge that none of us have been sent into this world to be idle.

In observing this truth, we can rest in knowing that God has delightfully given every man, woman, boy and girl an adeptness to work with, to be to Him for a name and praise in the earth that He might be glorified in the saints*!*

Tell me, what was Adam to do? How was he going to fulfill God's instructions given to him? Will he be shaken and become overwhelmed to handle such an enormous responsibility that could have discouraged him to cave in and quit on God?

Let's attend to God's Word and find out how Adam handled his responsibility as he made himself available and ready to serve God in this capacity.

Notice once again very carefully God's directive:

> "Then the Lord God took the man and put him in the garden of Eden to **tend (dress)**- *enhance, to grow, to expand, to increase, build up and to embellish"* and **keep it.** "   Genesis 2:15

This great responsibility given to them I imagine was somewhat arduous to do because after all, we would like to believe and think in our minds that the Garden was already perfectly flawless, showing no signs of having need to be upgraded, revamped or made more beautified than what it was.

But surprisingly, we have thus learned that there was something more obvious that God desired to develop in the lives of both Adam and Eve as they obeyed in fulfilling this assignment. Remember, as I stated before-God is a God of Covenant and He will never ask you to do anything that He is not willing to do Himself!

We must follow His example and be willing to carry out the command of His Word that is spoken to us without wavering and furthermore, learn to rest in His sovereignty and leadership.

Just think for a moment, if Adam had not been faithful to carry out the will of The Father as he was charged,
"What would have happened to the conditions of the land and how would it have affected his relationship with God?"
Looking from a farmer's point of view had Adam and Eve *not* kept God's command in properly manicuring the Garden, the lesser possibility of them harvesting any gain would have resulted zero return.

In obedience to God's will, Adam industriously carried out God's command without hesitation.
His expertise skill to farm-(*cultivate, tend, embellish, enhance, protect and maintain*) the Garden contributed much to his success rate in receiving benefit of his actions that yielded him a harvest that was endlessly abundant and complete!

"Have you put aside an assignment that God has placed in your hands to do? "Are there moments in your life when you become overwhelmed and you feel like just throwing in the towel and giving up on the plans that He has showed you? Whatever comes your way do not give up, instead be encouraged and reach out to God!

> "Be not deceived; God is not mocked:
> for whatsoever a man soweth, that shall
> he also reap. For he that sows to his flesh
> shall of the flesh reap corruption; but he
> that soweth to the Spirit shall of the Spirit
> reap life everlasting and let us not be weary in
> well doing: for in due season we shall reap,
> if we faint not." Galatians 6:-7-9 KJV

We can learn another interesting Biblical truth that also explicitly divulges God's other intention for the purposes of Divine "preparation" as mentioned in Ephesians 2:10. Let's read together God's vision plan that He has sculptured for our lives.

> "We are God's own handiwork, recreated
> in Christ Jesus, (born anew) that we may
> do those good works which God
> predestined (*planned beforehand*)-for us
> (taking paths which He *prepared* ahead
> of time), that we should walk in them
> (living the good life which He *prearranged*
> and made ready for us to live." **[AMP]**

The Greek word for "workmanship" used in this particular text is "POIEMA," which is the English word for poem and poetry that has been defined as "that which is made" according to Vine's Expository Dictionary.

In essence, You and I are considered to be God's very own masterpieces-uniquely and chiefly designed, hand crafted and molded into a work of art that distinctively utters from the mouth of God, that we are His canvased, prized possessions and His showcases of delightful poems!

In moving forward, let's define the simple definition given for the word *preparation*.

The word KUWN-(koon) in the Hebrew language for preparation means to be *firm, be stable, to be securely determined, to be set up, or to make ready* in accordance to Strong's Concordance.

When I glare at this definition given, I find myself more and more in awe of God and His Impeccable Character.

Did you notice in this definition that every verb that is used to describe *preparation* matches God's Master Plan in guiding us to accomplishing His purpose in our lives?

The first verb given in defining the word preparation clearly informs us that we must be firm, secure, *strong*, certain, positive and well- grounded.

The scripture that comes to mind resembling this spiritual trait is mentioned in Ephesians 6:10 declaring:

> "Finally, my brethren, be *strong* in the Lord
> and in the power of His might."

This spiritual weapon which God has provided for us best deters the opposing forces of the enemy's attacks.

So stand strong in faith, and remain strong in His grace and God will avenge those that trusts in Him and cause you to be triumphant no matter the test!

> "Now thanks be unto God, which always causes
> us to triumph in Christ, and makes manifest
> the savor of His knowledge by us in every place."
> II Corinthians 2:14

The very next verb given to define preparation is that we are to be stable, or better yet to be unwavering, constant, *established*, and to be *steady* and sound in our faith walk at all costs.

A perfect example of this would be the blessed, fortunate man who fears and reveres the Lord that is found in the 112th division of Psalm.

This is one of my favorite scriptures God lead me to mediate on and to mutter over through the years in my Christian walk-and the peace that I have gained from this promise has indeed transformed my life.

"Have you located this scripture in your Bible yet?

If so, let's begin to take a look and see what God says about you as we study these passages in the book of Psalm 112:6-8 **[AMP]** *[Italicized for Emphasis]*

> "This man will not be moved forever,
> the uncompromisingly righteous-
> **[Brackets Mine] [Those in right standing with God]**shall be in everlasting remembrance. His heart is firmly fixed, trusting on and being confident in the Lord, he is *established* and *steady*."

A steady heart in the Hebrew poems, where "heart" means "mind" can easily be translated in this text of scripture as one who does not alter, deviate or changes his/her mind about the goodness of God.

The surest way of establishing the heart is to trust in the Lord. When a man or woman have a clear and better understanding of who they are it becomes easy for them to fulfill God's purpose for their lives by committing to live a life of complete trust in the Lord.

Another great scripture that speaks clearly to us about preparation in a more practical way from God's perspective is versed in the book of Proverbs 24:27 and it recites:

> "Prepare your work without and make it fit
> for yourself in the field; and afterwards
> build your house."

I want you to observe carefully what the Psalmist, David was trying to convey to the reader, as he mentions the different ways as to how we should apply wisdom to gain and achieve success in our endeavors as it pertains to *"preparation."*

Obviously, this proverb bids the believer to:
1) Attend first to those things which takes precedence over the menial details of other matters in our busy lives.

In other words, a better example of this would be to secure your *source* of income before you take on more responsibility that will demand more spending
(See Luke 14:28-30).
.

The next important observation of passage gives very practical advice bidding the believer to literally:
2) Make sure that you are well rooted, grounded and established in the areas of your profession prior to committing to deeper obligations before you take on greater responsibilities.

The very last verse in this passage of scripture provides the believer with this proper advice bidding him to:
3) To be faithful with the little first and God will bring the increase in your life at His appointed time.

The Bible tells us that "though our beginnings be small, yet our latter end shall greatly be increased."   Job 8:7

We can definitely mirror our lives accordingly by following the teachings of this proverbial saying in many forms.

Typically when we talk about preparedness as it applies to one's personal affairs in life, a wise action plan that is executed in a believer's life oftentimes, becomes the formula or the blueprint by which he/she uses as a projector towards reaching and achieving their goals.

Let this same mindset be one that you will execute in your personal relationship with God as you seek His counsel, His wisdom, His instructions and of course, His guidance in achieving your goals in life!

God has called you to greatness, so follow His lead and He will direct your footsteps to tread on new territories that He has already *prearranged, predestined, prepared and made ready* just for you!

The question is, will you be willing to lay down countless tasks at the "drop of a hat" in complete obedience to God when He enquires you to heed to His command?

Let's revisit the story of Abraham, the Father of Faith, the one whom God commanded to take his only son, Isaac,
to go to the land of Moriah to sacrifice him as a burnt offering on the mountain that God had chosen.
God had given Abraham all of the specific details as to what he had to do prior in advance as he was being *prepared* to offer up his son to God.

    Follow me search the scriptures to dig a little deeper than we did previously and highlight every action that was taken in obedience towards Abraham executing this command.

The story first tells us that Abraham *rose up early* in the morning, he *saddled his donkey*, and *took two* of his young *men* with him, and *clave to the wood* for the burnt offering and *went unto the place* of which God had instructed.

Notice very carefully, in the next few passages of scriptures how Abraham operated in the purest form of *expectation*. Genesis 22, Abraham said to his servants: "Stay here with the donkey and while I and the boy go over there.
We will worship and *then we will come back* to you."
(verse 5.)   [*Italicized for Emphasis*]

Abraham said to Isaac as he prepared the fire and the wood: "God will provide the lamb for the burnt offering," and when they reached the place God had told him about, Abraham built the altar there and arranged the wood on it.

He bound his son Isaac and laid him on the altar, on top of the wood. Then he reached out his hand and took the knife to slay his son. But the angel of the Lord called out to him from heaven, "Abraham! Abraham!"

The angel spoke and told him not to lay a hand on the boy and not to slay him.

The Bible tells us that Abraham looked up and there in the thicket he saw a ram caught by its horn and later took the ram and sacrificed it as a burning offering instead of his son.

Did you catch a glimpse of this portrait-God not only provided a ram in the bush but that He also acted in response to Abraham's *prepared heart* of obedience through faith that exceeded his expectations by leaps and bounds in sparing his son's life!

Abraham chose to demonstrate by his actions taken that he could trust God and to believe without doubt what God had spoken to him.

This clear evidence we have of his determined, steadfast and unshakeable faith is to be greatly admired and highly esteemed in the Body of Christ.

Because of the covenant he had made with God, Abraham was more than sure that God would intervene and in fact, provide another sacrificial offering than to sacrifice Isaac, the seed of promise.

Abraham sought to please God above all else and trusted Him with all of his being. He was able to stay connected to God and depend on the comfort of the precious promises that God would meet all of his needs by making every provision possible that he ever needed for him and his son, Isaac.

Abraham's mindset to remaining steadfast, and the grace to move at God's promptings were training opportunities that had been designed solely for him to develop a deep dependence on The Father.

These challenging times that Abraham experienced on Mount Moriah magnified his keen awareness to yearn for God's help and mercy during those moments of adversity.
Abraham, the Father of Faith and the Friend to God, set before us all such an illustrative paradigm to follow which guarantees that you and I can do all things through Christ that strengthens us when we set our will to believe!

(See Philippians 4:13.)

As we come to a close of this chapter it is my desire to both encourage and to uplift you to stay in *expectation*.

Many of God's greatest works here on earth are through those individuals that are willing to trust, praise and believe on Him.
For those that have remained in the state of *expectancy* and not yet received the fruit of your prayers the encouragement I give to you is to; wait patiently on The Lord, your God and to persevere by continuing on *in faith*.

Remember, God's timetable is not our timing and He knows the exact hour and day of our victory.

I want you to put down this book for just a moment and after you have finished reading the next few paragraphs- take a deep breath, keep your eyes fastened on God, lift up your hands to the Lord by asking Him to show you a glimpse of you running *your* race and going through the finish line.

With careful thought given to this next question, I would ask that you once more begin to use your vivid and creative imagination by envisioning what promptings were given to you by the Holy Spirit to get in shape to *prepare* for this amazing race?

After this is done, now see yourself entering your race for a worthy cause to "break free" from sickness and disease, financial debts, drug and sexual addictions, phobias, envies, mental disorders, bitterness, resentment, strife, the venom of un-forgiveness and any other stronghold that Satan has attempted to use as a weapon against you.

As you draw near to the end of your race and set your sight on the finished course, begin to raise up your hands high to the Lord, bringing Him your very best in offering the highest sacrifices of thanksgiving and praise!

So finally, as you press in and press forward-be most assured that God, who is the Judge of this race, will be there at the finish line to celebrate your great victory, as He gives you a round hand of applause and place the gold medallion around your neck as you bow down before Him for all the world to see!

A bona fide Champion is most Indicative of You!

He is above all, *The Author* and *The Finisher To Your Faith*!

Last but not least, today I want to encourage you to take the first initial step of walking in your freedom by asking God to show you His very best that He has to offer you?

I believe God's tender response in your quest to this childlike question will be:

"I gave You My very best when I gave You My Son, Jesus Christ!"

Chapter 6. *R* .. "*R*emarkable *R*esults"

*"Now therefore stand and see this great thing
that the Lord will do before your eyes."*
I Samuel 12: verse 16

In reflection upon what we have learned thus far with such studies, from **P**racticing the Presence of God as we **R**each towards Heaven to Relate to the **A**lmighty God by **Y**ielding and preparing to receive with **E**xpectation from Him, please allow me to share with you in the finale of this passionate journey to *Prayer* some of the most notoriously Astounding, Astonishing, Amazing, Admirable and most Wondrous, **R**emarkable Results that divinely highlights the Sovereignty of our Great and Mighty God.
Please come join me as we salute *The King of Kings, The Lord of Lords* and *The Son of The Living God, Jesus*, as we stand in acclamation of the Great and Mighty wonders that He has accomplished in the lives of those God-fearing men and women in Bible history that fostered righteously their belief in Him to be as their Savior, Lord, Defender, Champion, Mighty Warrior, Judge, Deliverer, Provider, Creator, Comforter, Confidant, Compass, Example, Teacher, Exhorter, Healer, Master, Sustainer, Protector, Preserver, God, Father and Closest Friend!
As we approach our study, we shall better understand the meaning of the statement that has oftentimes been said;
"If we had a million tongues to describe God-words could not possibly contain nor echo all that He truly is."

In these next few powerful moving pages you will find after each Biblical sequel to some of the stories shared, scriptural references I have carefully selected to provide additional research for you, the reader.

As you mediate on these great victories that have been chosen to display The Sovereignty of God, it is my earnest desire that you will passionately invite praise to join you at His throne, and to summon worship to echo its voice in tender affection that is accompanied with gaiety, as a virtuous expression of heartfelt responses in your admiration of God's Omniscient Existence to His resplendent and glorious Omnipotent power!

Let's begin by taking a look at how God made and created everything that He first willed by calling the heaven and earth into existence by upholding all things by the word of His power. (See Hebrews 1:3.)

"Through faith we understand that the worlds were framed by the word of God so that things which are seen were not made of things which do appear."

Hebrews 11:3

This world in which we now live at one time is described in the book of Genesis as being a place that was once hollow, empty, void, uninhabited, unoccupied, and bare.

The account in Genesis also records that God used words like; **"Said"** and **"Let there be"** to create such beauty that reflects some of the vastness of who He is.

These same two powerful words repeatedly echoed by God in the activity of creating Heaven and earth and all of its splendor were indeed the *Remarkable Results* of His Sovereignty that penetrated this earth with the glorious Light of His Presence!

God said, **"Let there be light and there was light."**

Genesis 1:3

God said, **"Let there be a firmament in the midst of the waters, and let it divide the waters from the waters."** God called the firmament Heaven and the evening and the morning were the second day.

Genesis 1:6, 8

God said these words mixed with faith, **"Let the waters under the heaven be gathered together unto one place and let the dry land appear and God called the dry land Earth and the gathering together of the waters called He Seas and God saw that it was good."**
Genesis 1:9-10

God said, **"Let the earth bring forth grass, the herb yielding seed, and the fruit tree yielding fruit after his kind whose seed is in itself; upon the earth and it was so."** Genesis 1:11

God said, **"Let there be lights in the firmament of the heaven to divide the day from the night and let them be for signs and for seasons and for days and years."**
Genesis 1:14

God said, **"Let the waters bring forth abundantly the moving creature that hath life and fowl that may fly above the earth in the open firmament of heaven."**
Genesis 1:20

God said, **"Let the earth bring forth the living creature after his kind…"** Genesis 1:24

God said, **"Let us make man in our own image, after our likeness and let them have dominion over the fish, of the sea and over the fowl of the air, and over the cattle, and over all the earth, and over every creeping thing that creeps upon the earth."** Genesis 1:26

God created both male and female and said unto them, **"Be fruitful and multiply and replenish the earth and subdue it and have dominion"….** Genesis 1:27-28

God said, **"Behold, I have given you every herb bearing seed which is upon the face of all the earth, and every tree, in which is the fruit of a tree yielding seed: for you it shall be for meat."** Genesis 1:29

As we sit quietly and begin to gaze in awe of God's Divine *Artistry in The Creation*, it impacts our lives in such a way that rightly justifies us, as His dear children to give our GOD all of the glory due unto His name and reverently worship Him in the beauty of holiness! (See Psalm 29:1-2.)

Come walk with me on another path that is considered to be Faith's Hall of Fame as we pay tribute by giving homage to those men and women, the "gladiators of faith," who looked to God as being their Redeemer, Lord and Friend.

All of the events mentioned below have been recorded as testimonies in Bible history that depicts the character of God's power. We will discover from these events of Biblical history that God's Word is alive!

We know that God's word declares in Hebrews 4:12 these words; "For the word that God speaks is alive and full of power [making it active, operative, energizing and effective; it is sharper than any two-edged sword, penetrating to the dividing line of the breath of life (soul) and the (immortal spirit.) and of joints and marrow of the deepest parts of our nature, exposing and sifting and analyzing and judging the very thoughts and purposes of the heart.

Let's take a close look at some of the phenomenal and *Remarkable Results* of how God's Word brought life and victory in the lives of our Forefathers in Bible history.
In order to provide further assistance in learning more about our Forefathers in Bible history, I have selected the book of Hebrews to serve as a tour guide that it might show us the way by leading us into Faith's Hall of Fame.
As we delve into Hebrews chapter 11:2-40 it firmly reinstates and accurately reminds us that our Forefathers lived by faith, trusted God and set standards that we too, must follow when making Jesus, our Lord and Savior!
These reports that you are about to read exposes the victories and the triumphs they experienced by trusting God with the impossible and believing on Him for the extraordinary outcomes of *Remarkable Results!*

Did you know Hebrews chapter 2 verse 4 says that because Abel had faith he offered God a better sacrifice than Cain did.

God was pleased with him and his gift, and even though Abel is now dead, his faith still speaks for him today.

Remarkable Results!   Genesis 4

Did you know Hebrews 11:5 says that Enoch had faith and was translated that he should not see death; and was not found, because God had translated him, for before his translation he had this testimony, that he pleased God.

Remarkable Results!   Genesis 5:24

Did you know that Hebrews 11:7 says Noah had faith, being of God of things not seen yet, moved with fear, prepared an ark to the saving of his house; by the which he condemned the world, and became heir of the righteousness which is by faith.

Remarkable Results!   Genesis 7:5-23, 8:1-18

Did you know that Hebrews 11:8 says Abraham had faith and when he was called to go out into a place which he should after receive for an inheritance, obeyed; and he went out, not knowing whither he went.

By faith he sojourned in the land of promise, as in a strange country, dwelling in tabernacles with Isaac and Jacob, the heirs with him of the same promise. For he looked for a city which hath foundations, whose builder and maker is God.

Remarkable Results!   Genesis 12, 13

There are no seemingly impossibilities where God is the nucleus of your faith!

Did you know that Hebrews 11:11 says through faith also Sara herself received strength to conceive seed, and was delivered of a child when she was past age, because she judged him faithful who had promised.

Remarkable Results! Genesis 21:1-3

Did you know Hebrews chapter 11 and verse 17 records that by faith, Abraham, when he was tried, offered up Isaac and he that had received the promises offered up his only begotten son, of whom it was said, That in Isaac shall thy seed be called; accounting that God was able to raise him up, even from the dead; from whence also he received him in a figure.

Did you know Hebrews 11:20 says Isaac had faith, and he blessed Jacob and Esau concerning things to come. By faith Jacob when he was dying, blessed both the sons of Joseph; and worshipped, leaning upon the top of his staff.

Remarkable Results! Genesis 49

Did you know Hebrews 11:23 says; By faith Moses, when he was born, was hid for three months of his parents, because they saw he was proper child; and they were not afraid of the king's commandment.

Remarkable Results! Exodus 2:1-3

Did you also know that Hebrews 11:24 says after Moses grew up he refused to be called the son of Pharaoh's daughter; choosing rather to suffer affliction with the people of God, than to enjoy the pleasures of sin for a season; esteeming the reproach of Christ greater riches than the treasures in Egypt; for he had respect unto the recompense of the reward.

Remarkable Results! Exodus 2:10-15

Because of his faith, Moses left Egypt not fearing the wrath of the king; for he endured, as seeing him who is invisible.

Through faith he kept the Passover, and the sprinkling of blood, lest he that destroyed the firstborn should touch them.

Remarkable Results! Exodus 12:22-29

Did you know Hebrews 11:29 says because of their faith, the people passed through the Red sea as by dry land; which the Egyptians assaying to do were drowned.

Remarkable Results! Exodus 14:21-25

The Bible records in Hebrews chapter 11 and verse 30 that by faith the walls of Jericho fell down, after they were compassed about seven days.

Remarkable Results! Joshua 6

Did you know Hebrews 11:31 tells us that by faith the harlot Rehab perished not with them that believed not, when she received the spies with peace.

Remarkable Results! Joshua 2

"What else can I say about His Delivering Power, His Awesome Mighty Strength, His Saving Grace, His Tender Mercies and His Interminable Agape Love that He has for you and for me?"

Tell me, "who" wouldn't serve a God like our Great Jehovah!

There is no other like Him, for He is The Lord, our Conquering King "who causes us to run through troops and leap over walls." Psalms 18:29

Follow along with me as the text continues to highlight the miraculous victories of those who both witnessed and experienced God's grace.

Among those mentioned were King David, Gideon, Barak, Samson, Jephthah [a judge over Israel], and Samuel [Son of Elkanah and Hannah].

The scripture reports their triumphs in this way as written….who through faith subdued kingdoms, wrought righteousness, obtained promises, stopped the mouth of lions, quenched the violence of fire, escaped the edge of the sword, out of weakness were made strong, waxed valiant in fight, turned to flight the armies of the aliens.

Remarkable Results!   Hebrews 11:33-34

Did you know it has been said for many believers that one of the greatest stories ever recorded in the Bible is the Crucifixion, burial and resurrection of our Lord and Savior, Jesus Christ.

Did you also know that while the executioners were piercing Jesus hands and his feet with nails, He calmly prayed for them and for those who had dealt hands in his death by asking God to forgive them by saying;

"Father, forgive them, for they know not what they do."

Truly this was the character of God's only-begotten Son, The One, who demonstrated love and mercy to a world that brutally crucified, mocked and rebelled against Him!

Remarkable Results!   (See Luke 23:34.)

Did you know when the soldiers had nailed Jesus naked body to the cross and raised him up on the cross, they divided His garments into four parts and cast lots for the shares that it might be fulfilled which was spoken by the prophet, they parted my garments among them, and upon my vesture did they cast lots.

Remarkable Results!   Matthew 27:35

Did you know that it was around the ninth hour when Jesus cried again with loud voice, yielded up the ghost and behold, the veil of the temple was rent in twain from the top to the bottom; and the earth did quake, and the rocks rent; and the graves were opened; and many bodies of the saints which slept arose, and came out of the graves after His resurrection, that they went into the holy city, and appeared unto many.

Remarkable Results! Matthew 27:50-53

Did you know when the evening had come after Jesus was placed in a tomb that was guarded by Roman soldiers that there came a rich man of, named Joseph , who also himself was Jesus' disciple; he went to Pilate and begged for the body of Jesus to be delivered.

Remarkable Results! Matthew 27:57

Did you know that when Joseph had taken the body he wrapped it in a clean linen cloth and laid it in his own new tomb and rolled a great stone to the door of the sepulcher and departed?

Remarkable Results! Matthew 27:59-60

Now the next day, that followed the day of the preparation, the chief priests and Pharisees came together unto Pilate saying, Sir we remember that the deceiver said, While He was yet alive, **after three days I will rise again**. They commanded that the sepulcher be made sure until the third day, lest His disciples came by night and steal Him away and say unto the people, He is Risen from the dead: so the last error shall be worse than the first.

So they went and made the sepulcher sure, sealing the stone, and setting a watch. Matthew 27:62-66

The record also bears witness at the end of the Sabbath, came Mary Magdalene and the other, Mary-the mother of James and Joses, to see the sepulcher and behold there was an earthquake and the angel of the Lord descended from heaven, and came and rolled back the stone from the door and sat upon it.

What was so remarkable about this truth is that the angel answered and said unto the women, "Fear not" for I know that you seek for Jesus, which was crucified, He is not here: for He is risen, as He said, Come see the place where the Lord lay." As the two women departed in great joy to run and share this word with the disciples, behold Jesus met them saying, **"All hail"** and they came and held him by the feet and worshipped Him.

Empathetically, Jesus saw their fear and calmed their doubts by the gentleness of His voice that melodiously exuded from out of His mouth. Jesus gave the women explicit instructions to tell the brethren what they had witnessed and to meet Him for His appearing in Galilee.

The scripture also tell us that they all went to Galilee into a mountain and when the disciples saw Jesus, they worshipped Him: but some even doubted if it was really Him.

Jesus knowing their thoughts, said these words:

> **"All power is given unto me in heaven and in earth. Go ye therefore, and teach all nations, baptizing them in the name of the Father, and of the Son, and of the Holy Ghost, teaching them to observe all things whatsoever I have commanded you: and lo, I am with you always even until the end of the world."   Amen**

Remarkable Results! (See Matthew 27-28.)

May the infallible truths of God's Word that has been presented and shared with you in writing this book intensely **impact** your life, **re-direct** your steps, **change** your thinking, and most importantly, ultimately **re-shape** your relationship with God, who has the power to **transform** you little by little into His likeness as you were crafted and distinctively purposed to be!

May His Loving Presence Forever Surround You Minute by Minute and Day by Day.
May You Come To Fully Understand and Experience The Purest Essential Ingredient To Staying Close To Him Through The Power
Of
"Prayer That Changes Things"

If you have enjoyed this book
and it has been an empowerment to your life,

I would love to hear from you.

Please send comments to

Prayer That Changes Things Book Feedback
at
ptctcomments @ gmail.com

Live To Love

www.ingramcontent.com/pod-product-compliance
Lightning Source LLC
Chambersburg PA
CBHW032033040426
42449CB00007B/875